MY BODY
Is Amazing!

Author
Tracy Edmunds, M.A. Ed.

Managing Editor
Mara Ellen Guckian

Editor in Chief
Brent L. Fox, M. Ed.

Creative Director
Sarah M. Fournier

Cover Artist
Diem Pascarella

Art Coordinator
Renée Mc Elwee

Illustrators
Wayne Potrue
Amanda R. Harter

Imaging
Amanda R. Harter

Publisher
Mary D. Smith

Teacher Created Resources
12621 Western Avenue
Garden Grove, CA 92841
www.teachercreated.com

ISBN: 978-1-4206-1755-9

©2023 Teacher Created Resources

Made in U.S.A.

For standards correlations, visit
http://www.teachercreated.com/standards/

Teacher Created Resources

Table of Contents

Introduction

The human body is amazing! Did you know you wake up each morning taller than when you went to bed? Or that your brain makes food taste better when you are hungry? Have you ever wondered what causes you to hiccup? Or just how much blood is in your body? Find out in this book!

Along with amazing facts, you'll learn how the different systems in your body work and how those systems work together to keep you alive and healthy.

There are lots of fun projects to try, too. Make "blood" in a jar and create a working model of your hand! Check out your own fingerprints and engineer a heart valve!

Get ready to learn all about your awesome, surprising, extraordinary body!

For parents and educators:

This fun and engaging book is filled with activities and ideas to stretch kids' thinking, expand their vocabularies, and get them engaged in learning. The focus is on their own bodies and how they work, with a good helping of amazing human body facts for them to learn along the way. Kids will interact with each page of the book by reading, writing, drawing, coloring, and more. There are also plenty of hands-on, minds-on activities and projects to try using common materials you have at home. Whether they are closely examining their own skin, experiencing optical illusions, or seeing how flexible they can be, kids will have many opportunities to discover the amazing workings of their bodies. Read and play along with your child—you just might learn something new!

TRY THIS!

This book uses a lot of grays, which do not always reproduce well. If you plan to duplicate pages on a photocopier, try using the machine's "Photo" setting to decrease the chance of some elements on the page copying too lightly.

What Are Cells?

Cells are the smallest living parts of your body. They are like tiny machines with lots of parts working together.

Directions: Color the cell. Most human cells have no color, so use your imagination!

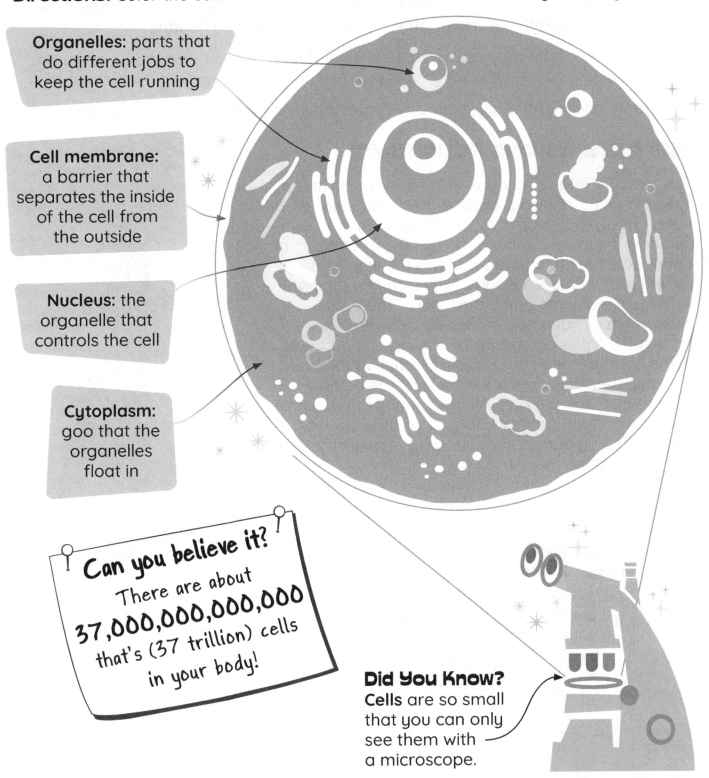

Organelles: parts that do different jobs to keep the cell running

Cell membrane: a barrier that separates the inside of the cell from the outside

Nucleus: the organelle that controls the cell

Cytoplasm: goo that the organelles float in

Can you believe it? There are about 37,000,000,000,000 that's (37 trillion) cells in your body!

Did You Know? Cells are so small that you can only see them with a microscope.

4

A Cell-tacular Treat

Recipe: Edible Cell Model

Ingredients

☐ gelatin

☐ fruit, sweets, or vegetables in different shapes:
  fruit: apples, oranges, blueberries
  sweets: cookies, jellybeans, fruit strips, marshmallows
  vegetables: carrot peels

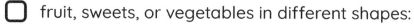

Directions

1. Make a bowl of gelatin according to the package directions. Put it in the refrigerator until it is wobbly. This will be the **cytoplasm** of your cell model.

2. Stick a round cookie or half an apple into the gelatin to make a **nucleus**.

3. Add **organelles** using the food ingredients. Look at the cell you colored to see their shapes.

   - Some organelles are round like blueberries or marshmallows.

   - Some organelles are wavy like carrot peels or fruit strips.

   - Some organelles are bean-shaped like orange sections or jellybeans.

WOW! About 10,000 red blood cells could fit on the head of a pin!

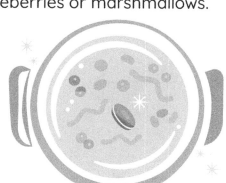

Ha ha!
What do you call it when a scientist takes a picture of herself?
A *cell*fie!

What did you use for each cell part?

cytoplasm: _____

nucleus: _____

organelles: _____

Cells Are Amazing

Red blood cells do not have nuclei.

Did you know? There are over **200** kinds of cells in your body.

red blood cells

nerve cell

skin cells

bone cell

muscle cells

Most cells **divide**. They split themselves in two to make more cells just like them. Below is an illustration of a skin cell dividing into two new skin cells. Skin cells divide frequently. This is one way your body grows and repairs itself.

Another way your body makes more cells is with **stem cells**. Stem cells are special because they can turn into other kinds of cells. All your blood cells started as stem cells inside your bones.

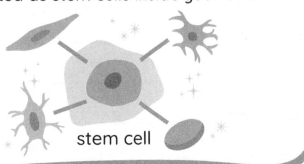

stem cell

Nerve cells are also special because they do *not* divide. You keep the same nerve cells your whole life.

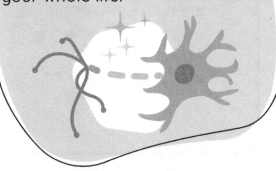

Sketch, Explore, Respond

Draw a skin cell.

Directions: Follow the maze through the cell to the nucleus.

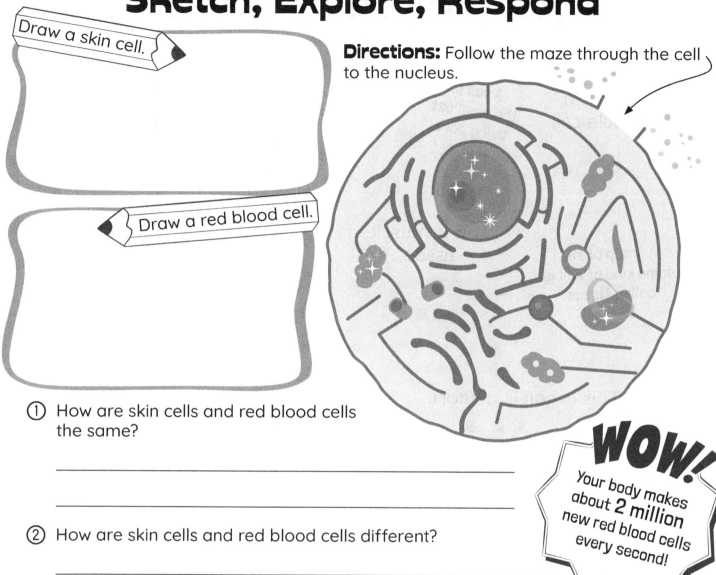

Draw a red blood cell.

① How are skin cells and red blood cells the same?

_____

_____

② How are skin cells and red blood cells different?

_____

_____

WOW!
Your body makes about **2 million** new red blood cells every second!

Draw a skin cell dividing.

This is a _____ cell dividing.

How Does It All Work?

This is a muscle cell.

A **cell** is the smallest living part of you.

TRY THIS! Make a fist. That is about the size of your heart!

A group of the same kind of cell is called **tissue**.

This is muscle tissue.

This organ is a heart.

The heart is part of the circulatory system.

Different kinds of tissues work together in **organs**.

It has muscle tissue, connective tissue, and nerve tissue.

WOW! Your heart beats about **100,000** times a day!

Organs work together in body **systems**.

This system moves blood around your body.

Show What You Know!

Directions: Fill in the blanks with the words in the Word Bank.

Word Bank

organ   tissue   cell   system

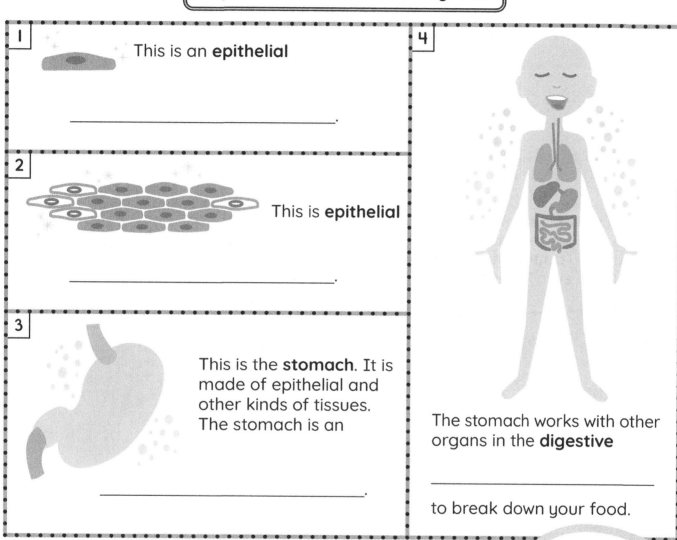

1 This is an **epithelial**

_____.

2 This is **epithelial**

_____.

3 This is the **stomach**. It is made of epithelial and other kinds of tissues. The stomach is an

_____.

4

The stomach works with other organs in the **digestive**

_____

to break down your food.

Your empty stomach is about the size of an apple.

Your stomach gets bigger as you fill it with food.

If you ate as much as you possibly could...

your stomach could expand to the size of a soccer ball!

Body Systems

➤ Your **muscular system** makes your body move.
➤ There are three kinds of muscles in your body. You can only control one kind. The others work without you even knowing!

➤ Your **skeletal system** provides structure for your body. Without it, you would be all wobbly, like jelly!

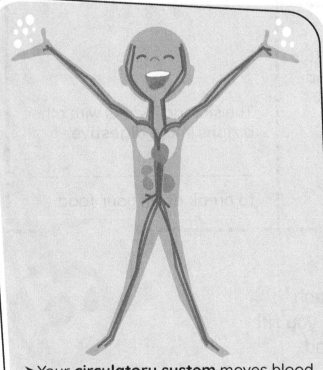

➤ Your **circulatory system** moves blood around your body.
➤ Blood brings oxygen and nutrients to all your cells. Your heart powers this system.

➤ Your **respiratory system** brings oxygen into your body and gets rid of carbon dioxide.
➤ This system's main organs are your lungs.

Body Systems *(cont.)*

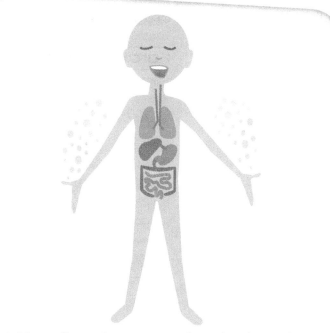

➤ Your **digestive system** breaks down food into tiny bits that your body can use and eliminates the rest.
➤ This system has lots of organs, including your stomach, liver, and intestines.

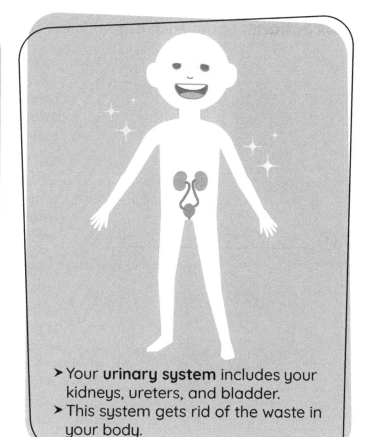

➤ Your **urinary system** includes your kidneys, ureters, and bladder.
➤ This system gets rid of the waste in your body.

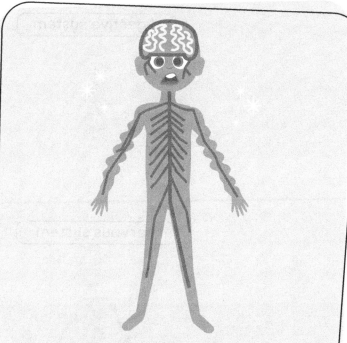

➤ Your **nervous system** controls your body.
➤ Signals go back and forth along your nerves from your brain to the rest of your body.

sight

smell

hearing

touch

taste

➤ Your **five senses** take information from the outside world and send it to your brain. Your brain acts on the information.

Organ to System Match

Directions: Label each organ. Then, draw a line to match each organ to its system.

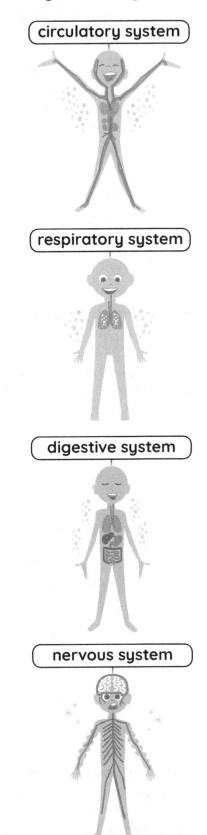

circulatory system

respiratory system

digestive system

nervous system

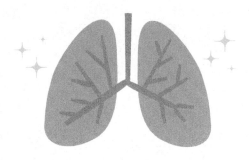

① _____

② _____

③ _____

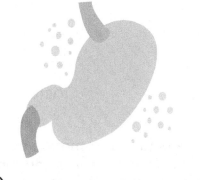

④ _____

Which System Is It?

Directions: Use the Word Bank to help you fill in the blanks.

Word Bank

circulatory   digestive   muscular   nervous   respiratory   skeletal

1. The _____ system moves blood around your body.

2. The system that controls your body is called the _____ system.

3. Your food is broken down by your _____ system.

4. The lungs are a part of the _____ system that brings oxygen into your body.

5. Without your _____ system, you would be soft and squishy all over.

6. You can move because you have a _____ system.

Ha ha!

How many bones are in a human body?

Hopefully, all of them!

The Great Protector

Can you say *Integumentary?* (in-teg-*yuh*-men-*tuh*-ree)

Your **integumentary** system is easy to see. It covers the outside of your body. Your skin, hair, and nails make up this important system.

Can you believe it?
You have about 20 square feet of skin. That's about the size of your bed! Your skin really is your largest organ!

Skin

Your skin is your biggest organ, and it has many jobs!

➤ It protects your body.

➤ It keeps out germs that can make you sick.

➤ It keeps you warm or cool.

Draw hair and nails, and color the skin.

Your skin is different all over your body.

➤ The thickest skin on your body is on the palms of your hands and the bottoms of your feet. It is around 1.5 millimeters thick, or about the thickness of a grain of rice.

➤ The thinnest skin on your body is around your eyes. It is only 0.2 millimeters thick.

Talk about it: Why do you think your skin is thicker on your hands and feet than it is around your eyes?

What Has Three Layers . . . ?

Did you know that your skin has three different layers? Take a look.

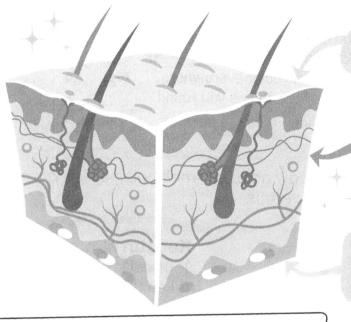

Epidermis: The outside layer that you can see and touch protects you.

Dermis: The middle layer has blood vessels, oil and sweat glands, and hair follicles.

Hypodermis: The inner layer connects to your bones and muscles. It has fat that keeps you warm.

Skin Activity 1: Magnify It

Materials

- ☐ white school glue
- ☐ soap and water or wipes
- ☐ magnifying glass
- ☐ craft sticks or spoons for spreading

Directions

1. Spread a thick layer of white glue on the palm of your hand and on the back of your hand. Try for a section that is about the size of a quarter.

2. Let the glue dry. It will be see-through, not white. It should take about 30 minutes. Try not to touch it while it is drying!

3. Gently pull at the edges and peel off the dried glue. Place it on a flat surface.

4. Look closely at the peeled side of the glue that touched your skin. What do you see? Use a magnifying glass to examine the dried glue.

5. Describe what you see. _____

_____

6. Wash your hands when you have completed the activity.

Outer Layer: Epidermis

TRY THIS!

Use a magnifying glass to look closely at your skin. Look at your skin on different parts of your body.
➤ Is your skin all the same?   **Yes   No**
➤ Is your skin the same color everywhere?   **Yes   No**
Check off the things you found.

☐ **freckles**   ☐ **hair**   ☐ **scar**   ☐ **scab**

You probably saw lines in your skin. Maybe you saw hairs or small holes called *pores*. You saw your outer layer of skin, called your *epidermis*.

Pores are small openings in your skin where sweat and oil come out.

The **cells** in your epidermis are like bricks in a brick wall. They help keep moisture in and bad things out.

Keratin is found in your cells. It is what makes the outer layer of your skin *tough* to protect you.

Your hair, fingernails, and toenails are made of keratin.

Melanin is at the bottom of the epidermis. It gives skin its color and protects it from sun damage. More melanin makes darker skin. Melanin also makes suntans and freckles.

Skin Activity 2: Check Your Prints

Materials: ☐ sharpened #2 pencil   ☐ two 2" squares of white paper   ☐ clear tape

1	Scribble hard with a pencil on a piece of paper so you have a small dark area. 	2	Rub one of your fingertips around in the dark area. 
3	Press your finger onto the sticky side of a piece of clear tape. Then, stick the tape on the second piece of white paper to see it even more clearly.		

Middle Layer: Dermis

The layer under your epidermis is called your **dermis**. It is much thicker than the epidermis. It has **collagen** in it, which makes it strong and stretchy. Each part of your dermis does a different job.

Oil glands make oil to keep your skin soft and protected.

Sweat glands make sweat to keep you cool.

Nerves tell your brain about what you feel touching your skin.

Blood vessels carry oxygen to the cells. They can also help keep you warm or cool.

Hair follicles make hairs.

A Quick Test

Directions: Put a little water on the back of your hand and blow on it. How does it feel?

The wet skin probably feels cooler than the rest of your skin. This is why we *sweat*. Sweat is made mostly of water.

➡ When our body gets hot, our brain tells our sweat glands to go to work.

➡ Sweat comes out of our **pores** and onto our skin.

➡ As the sweat evaporates from our skin, we cool down.

Lower Layer: Hypodermis

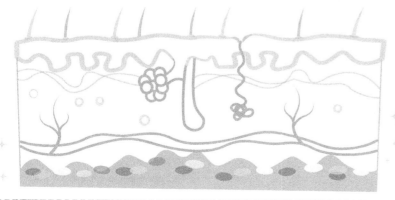

The deepest layer of skin is the **hypodermis**.

➤ It connects your skin to your muscles and bones.

➤ It stores fat that keeps you warm and that your body can use for energy.

17

Edible Treat

Recipe: Edible Skin Model

Ingredients

☐ mini marshmallows or banana slices ☐ skinny red licorice strings
☐ pudding or yogurt ☐ skinny black licorice strings
☐ graham crackers ☐ small candies or grapes

Materials

☐ clear plastic cups (8 oz.) ☐ spoons ☐ scissors

Directions

1. First, make the fatty **hypodermis**. It keeps you warm and connects your skin to your body.

   ➡ Place mini marshmallows or banana slices in the bottom of a clear plastic cup.

2. Next, make the **dermis**—the thick, middle layer of your skin.

   ➡ Add a thick layer of pudding or yogurt on top of the marshmallows or bananas.

   ➡ Add some skinny red licorice strings. These will represent the *blood vessels*.

   ➡ Add small candies or grapes. These will be the *sweat glands* and *oil glands*.

3. Then, make the **epidermis**—the thin, outer layer of your skin.

   ➡ Break up some graham crackers into small pieces and sprinkle a shallow layer on top of the "dermis."

4. Poke a few black licorice strings through the graham crackers into the pudding. These will represent hairs that grow from the dermis through the epidermis.

5. Finally, eat your edible treat!

Superhero Skin

Directions: Put a check mark next to the things your skin does for you.

What does skin do?

- ☐ protects your body
- ☐ keeps moisture in
- ☐ pumps your blood
- ☐ keeps germs and viruses out
- ☐ helps you feel heat and pain
- ☐ digests your food
- ☐ keeps your temperature from going too high or too low
- ☐ brings oxygen to your cells
- ☐ grows hair

Did you know that cells at the surface of your epidermis die and shed, or fall off, constantly? New cells form at the bottom of the epidermis and move up to take the place of the cells that have been shed. A new cell takes about a month to reach the top of the epidermis. That means your outer layer of skin gets replaced about once a month!

WOW!

The skin cells that shed off your body make about two pounds of dust each year!

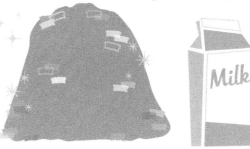

Two pounds of skin cells would weigh about the same as a quart of milk.

Ouch!

Have you ever gotten a cut or scrape? If so, you know that your skin can repair itself. It forms a **scab** to protect the area. Underneath the scab your skin works to heal itself. If the damage is bad, it will form a **scar**. Scar tissue can be a different color from the skin around it. It has no sweat glands or hair follicles.

Directions: Write ideas or draw pictures. In the "no" symbol, draw or write about two things you should *not* touch. In the hand, draw or write about items that are safe to touch.

Do not touch!   **OK to touch.**

Nerves in your skin help you feel heat and pain. For example, if you get near or touch something that is hot, the nerves in your hand send a message to your brain. You pull your hand away. This all happens before you even know you are doing it!

Message to brain: HOT   **Message from brain:** STOP TOUCHING!

Watch Out! UV Rays

Have you ever gotten a sunburn? It hurts! The UV rays from the sun can be a problem. Too much sun can damage your skin. It can damage the cells in your **epidermis** and **dermis**, even if you don't feel it. Sunburns can even happen on cloudy days!

Directions: Draw a box around the child who is protected from sun damage. Circle the items protecting the child from sun damage.

Tip
Wear sunscreen to protect your skin layers from sun damage.

Skin Activity 3: Sunscreen Test

Materials ☐ sunscreen ☐ dark blue or black construction paper

Directions

1. Fold a piece of dark-colored construction paper in half and unfold it again. Lay it flat.

2. Write "sunscreen" on one side of the fold line and "no sunscreen" on the other side of the fold line.

3. Rub sunscreen on the "sunscreen" side of the paper.

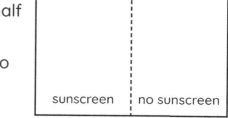

sunscreen ┊ no sunscreen

4. Place the paper out in the sun for a couple of hours. Log your start and end times.

Start Time: _____:_____   **End Time:** _____:_____

Observe: What happened to the paper?

_____

Why do you think this happened?

_____

Name Those Nails

Your fingernails and toenails are also part of your integumentary system. Nails are important.

➤ Nails protect the ends of your fingers and toes.

➤ Your fingernails help you pick things up.

➤ Fingernails can also scratch an itch, but be careful!

Did you know? The cells in your nails and hair are **dead**. That's why it doesn't hurt to cut them!

Use a marker to trace the cuticles. Color the nails if you wish.

Your **cuticle** is where your nail meets your skin.

Another word for your big toe is your **hallux**.

WOW! The world record for the longest fingernail is over **4 feet long**!

TRY THIS!

1. Get help taping a long straw to each finger.

2. Now try to pick things up or write.

3. Imagine having 4 straws taped together on each finger!

4. Would you like it? Why or why not?

_____

_____

Hair

Your hair is also part of your integumentary system. It is formed in **hair follicles** in your **dermis**. One hair forms at the base of each follicle and grows up through the follicle's tube. As the hair gets longer, it comes through your epidermis and out where you can see it. Isn't that amazing?

The hair on your head helps keep you warm and protects your head from the sun.

Draw eyes and eyebrows.

Eyelashes and eyebrows help keep dust and sweat out of your eyes.

Add eyelashes.

Directions

✎ Draw your hair on one side the head.

✎ On the other side, draw what you think your hair will look like when you are 50 years old.

Did you know?

Your hair color comes from **melanin**. When people get older, they lose the melanin in their hair, so it looks gray.

The way your hair grows from your hair follicles determines whether it's thick, thin, curly, or straight.

hair follicle

hair root

hair bulb

Hair can grow about half an inch per month. Each hair on your head grows for about 2 to 6 years. Then it rests for a few months and finally falls out.

Hair on your body helps keep you warm. It also helps you know if a bug is on you!

What Holds You Up?

Teamwork makes your body work! Your **skeletal system** and your **muscular system** are a team.

They work together to:

hold you up · hold you together

make you move

TRY THIS!

Open your hand.

Muscles used: **9**

Close your hand.

Muscles used: **9**

You just used **18 muscles!**

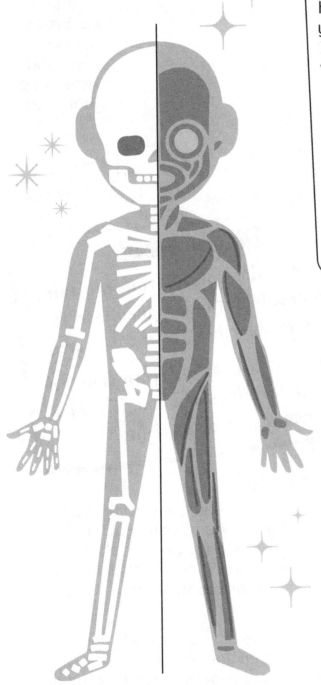

Your **skeleton** is made of bones. Bones are hard, and they give your body its shape. Imagine your body without bones . . . you would be a pile of goo on the floor!

Name three different bones you know:

_____

_____

_____

Muscles attach to other muscles and to your bones. Muscles *pull* to make you move, but they do not *push*. If you had a skeleton, but no muscles to move your bones, you would be stiff like a statue.

Some muscles do important jobs on their own without you ever thinking about it:

➤ Your **heart muscle** moves blood through your body.

➤ Smooth muscles in your **intestines** move food through your digestive system.

Name three muscles you know:

_____

_____

_____

_____

Your Skeleton

We all have a dancing skeleton inside our bodies! Your **skeleton** or **skeletal system** provides structure for your body. Your bones hold up all the other parts of you and they protect your **organs**.

How many bones do you have? You were born with about **300**. As you grow, some of your bones **fuse**, or join together.

Since everyone grows at their own pace, you might not have the same number of bones as your friends. When you are between the ages of 17 and 25, you will be done growing and you will have **206** bones.

WOW!

Bones are unusual in the animal world. Only about **4%** of animal species have bones!

96% Invertebrates animals without bones

4% Vertebrates animals with bones

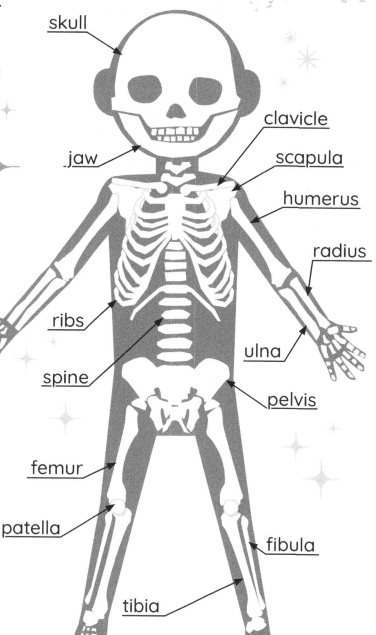

- skull
- clavicle
- scapula
- humerus
- jaw
- radius
- ribs
- ulna
- spine
- pelvis
- femur
- patella
- fibula
- tibia

RED — Color the *skull* and *jaw* red.

BLUE — Color the *shoulder*, *arm*, and *hand* bones blue. Read the scientific names for each body part.

GREEN — Color the *ribs* and *spine* green.

ORANGE — Color the *pelvis*, *leg*, and *foot* bones orange. Read the scientific names for each body part.

About Your Bones

Your bones are alive! They are made of living cells. They can grow and they can break. If they get broken, they can mend themselves back together.

Bones have **blood vessels** and **nerves**. Blood flow helps bones grow, heal, and stay healthy.

The outside of your bones is made of **compact bone**. It is hard and smooth. When you see a skeleton, you are seeing compact bone.

Inside is **spongy bone**. It has little holes and spaces in it, like a sponge. It is lighter and more flexible than compact bone, but it is still strong.

Bone marrow is in the hollow middle of a bone. It also fills up the spaces in spongy bone. Bone marrow is thick and gooey. It makes new blood cells for your body.

Directions: Use the bold words from above to fill in the labels on the diagram below.

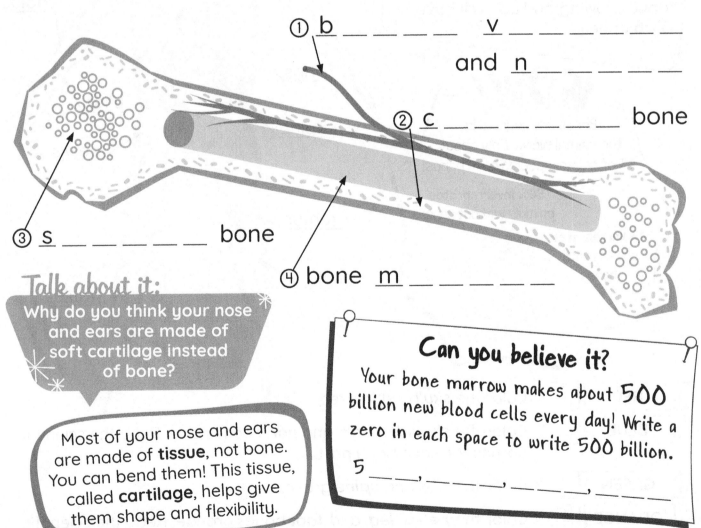

① b _ _ _ _   v _ _ _ _ _ _
and n _ _ _ _ _ _

② c _ _ _ _ _ _ _ bone

③ s _ _ _ _ _ _ bone

④ bone m _ _ _ _ _ _

Talk about it:

Why do you think your nose and ears are made of soft cartilage instead of bone?

Most of your nose and ears are made of **tissue**, not bone. You can bend them! This tissue, called **cartilage**, helps give them shape and flexibility.

Can you believe it?

Your bone marrow makes about 500 billion new blood cells every day! Write a zero in each space to write 500 billion.

5 _ _ _ , _ _ _ , _ _ _ , _ _ _

Your Skull

TRY THIS! Touch the top of your head. You can feel your skull!

Your **skull** is made of many bones. It is very important because it protects your brain. The top part of your skull is called the **cranium**. It is made of **8** separate bones that fuse together as you grow older.

Directions: Color each bone of the cranium a different color.

Your face has **14** bones. Most of them are in pairs, one on each side of the face.

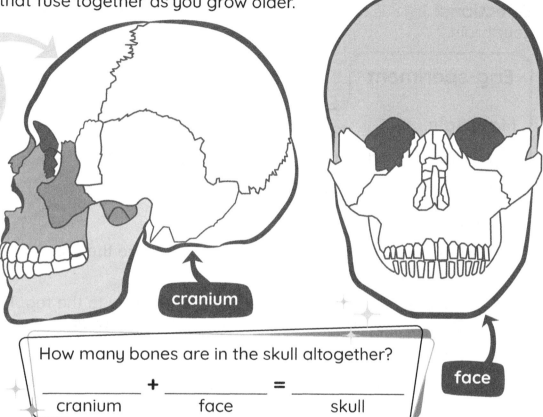

cranium

face

How many bones are in the skull altogether?

_____ + _____ = _____
cranium   face   skull

What is the only bone in your skull that moves? *Hint:* It allows you to eat.

_____

Did you know that there are tiny holes in your skull for blood vessels and nerves to pass through? This way, blood and messages can get *to* and *from* the brain.

Directions: Put a check mark next to activities where it is important to wear a helmet to protect your skull. Can you name others?

Protect Your Brain!

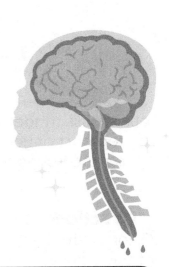

If you get hit in the head, or if you fall and bang your head, your hard skull takes the hit, keeping your soft brain safe inside. But your skull doesn't work alone. Your brain is surrounded by a **fluid** inside your skull. This clear liquid also surrounds your spinal cord.

Directions: Try this activity to see how the fluid helps to protect your brain.

Egg-speriment

Materials

☐ 2 raw, uncracked eggs   ☐ water

☐ 2 clear plastic containers with lids

Directions

1. Put an egg in each container. The eggs will be the brains and the containers will be the skulls.

2. Fill one of the containers with water all the way to the top. The water will represent the fluid surrounding your brain.

3. Put the lids on both containers. Check that they are closed tightly.

4. Hold one container in each hand, and shake those brains!

5. Set the containers down and observe them.

Draw what happened to the eggs.

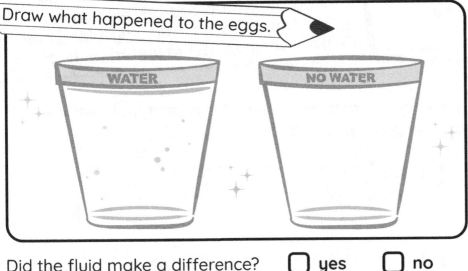

WATER   NO WATER

Why do you think this happened?

_____

_____

_____

_____

_____

_____

_____

Did the fluid make a difference?   ☐ **yes**   ☐ **no**

If yes, how? _____

Your Spine

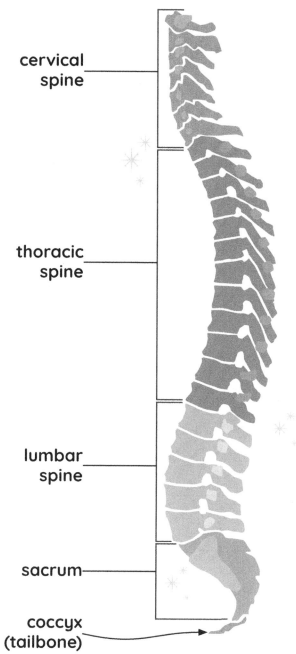

cervical spine

thoracic spine

lumbar spine

sacrum

coccyx (tailbone)

☐ bones in the neck

☐ bones in the chest

☐ bones in the lower back

1 — 5 fused vertebrae

1 — 4 fused vertebrae

Directions:
Count the vertebrae in the top 3 sections and fill in the blanks. Notice that the two groups of vertebrae at the bottom of the adult spine are fused.

Your **spine**, or **spinal column**, runs from the base of your skull down to your hips. It is sometimes called your **backbone**. Reach around to the middle of your back. Can you feel your backbone?

Your spine is made of bones, called **vertebrae**, stacked on top of each other.

Adults have 26 vertebrae. Doctors group them into five sections.

Gravity is always pulling on your body, causing your vertebrae to squish together. Every morning you wake up $\frac{1}{2}$ to $1\frac{1}{2}$ inches taller than you were when you went to bed. And your skeleton will shrink by 2 inches between ages 30 and 70!

0
1"
2"

Did you know astronaut Scott Kelly was **2 inches taller** when he returned to Earth after spending a year in the space station with zero gravity. Amazing! He did go back to his original height a few days after landing back on Earth.

Your Spine (cont.)

Directions: Read about the parts of your spine. Then, use the bold words to fill in the labels below the diagram. Color the **discs** blue, the **ligaments** green, and the **vertebrae** yellow.

Between each of your vertebrae there is a squishy part called a **disc**. Your discs cushion the **vertebrae** so they don't rub together as you move.

Your vertebrae are held together by tough, stretchy **ligaments** that run down the length of your spine. This lets your spine bend and twist and still keep its shape.

Your **spinal cord** runs from your brain down through the center of your spine. It carries messages from the brain to nerves that go out to the rest of your body. Your vertebrae protect your spinal cord.

① __ __ __ c

② __ __ __ __ __ __ __ __ a __

③ __ __ g __ __ __ __ __

④ __ __ __ __ __ __ c __ __ __

TRY THIS!

Nod your head up and down and turn it left and right. Keep your feet still and gently twist your upper body to look behind you. Bend over and touch your toes.

How else can you bend and twist your spine?

Amazing!

You have 7 neck bones, and so does a giraffe! Most mammals have 7 neck vertebrae, including whales. A giraffe's neck vertebrae are just much larger and longer than yours.

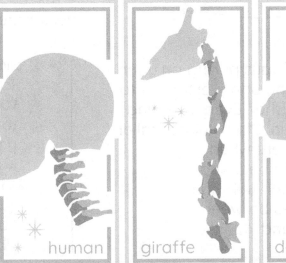

human   giraffe   dog

Spine-a-licious

Recipe: Edible Spine

Materials

- ☐ licorice strings for the spinal cord and nerves
- ☐ hard candies with a hole in the center or wheel-shaped pasta for the vertebrae
- ☐ soft candies with a hole in the center for the discs

Directions

1. Tie a hard candy *vertebra* onto the end of the licorice string *spinal cord*. This will keep everything from sliding off the end.
   - ➡ Your real vertebrae are made of bone and help protect your spinal cord.
   - ➡ You are born with 33 vertebrae and will have 26 by the time you are an adult.

2. Thread a soft candy *disc* onto the spinal cord and move it down next to the vertebra.
   - ➡ The flexible discs between your vertebrae allow you to bend and twist without pain.

3. Continue to stack vertebrae and discs onto the spinal cord in an alternating pattern.

4. Cut small sections of licorice strings and place two sticking out between each disc and vertebra.
   - ➡ These will be the *nerves* coming from your spinal cord to carry messages out to the rest of your body.

5. Try bending, flexing, and twisting your edible spinal cord. Can you make the same movements with your own body?

Craft Material Alternative: Use egg carton sections for the vertebrae; paper, foam, or felt circles for the discs; and yarn for the spinal cord and nerves.

Hands and Feet

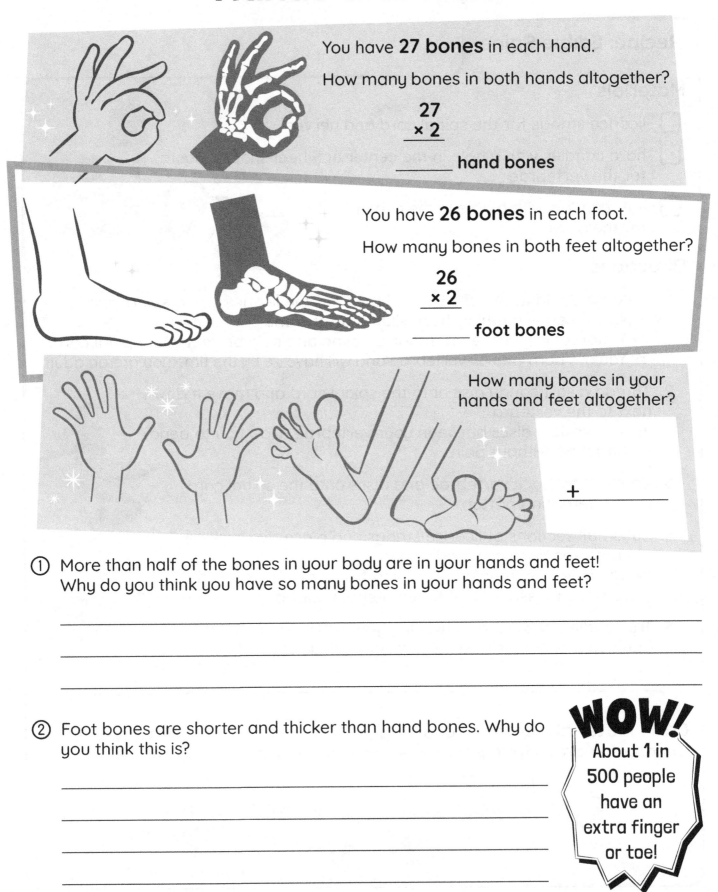

You have **27 bones** in each hand.

How many bones in both hands altogether?

$$\begin{array}{r} 27 \\ \times\ 2 \\ \hline \end{array}$$

_____ hand bones

You have **26 bones** in each foot.

How many bones in both feet altogether?

$$\begin{array}{r} 26 \\ \times\ 2 \\ \hline \end{array}$$

_____ foot bones

How many bones in your hands and feet altogether?

$$\begin{array}{r} \\ +\ \underline{} \\ \end{array}$$

① More than half of the bones in your body are in your hands and feet! Why do you think you have so many bones in your hands and feet?

_____

_____

_____

② Foot bones are shorter and thicker than hand bones. Why do you think this is?

_____

_____

_____

_____

WOW!

About 1 in 500 people have an extra finger or toe!

Your Joints

TRY THIS! Bend your elbow. Wiggle your fingers. Kick your leg. All of these movements are possible because of your joints!

A **joint** is where two bones come together. **Cartilage** covers the end of your bones and cushions your joints! Most joints allow you to bend and move your skeleton.

There are different kinds of joints in your body.

Fixed joint—The bones in your skull come together along **fixed joints**. You can't move them at all.

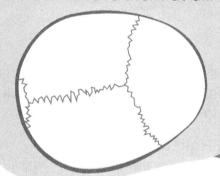

Hinge joint—Your elbow and knee are **hinge joints**. They can only bend one way.

Try bending your elbow to the side or backward. Unless you are double-jointed, you can't do it!

Ball-and-socket joint—Your hips and shoulders are **ball-and-socket joints**. They allow your arms and legs to move in lots of directions.

Make big circles with your arms. Your shoulder joints allow you to move your arms up, down, and side to side.

Directions: Write the correct type of joint for each body part on the lines below.

> hinge joint
> ball-and-socket joint
> fixed joint

shoulder _____

cranium _____

knee _____

Long, Strong, and Stretchy

You have lots of **connective tissues** in your body. They are long, strong, and stretchy. These tissues have different jobs.

Ligaments are like rubber bands. They attach bones to other bones at joints. They are strong to hold the bones together, and also stretchy so the bones can move.

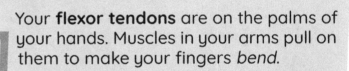

Tendons attach your **muscles** to your bones. When the muscles contract (get shorter), they pull on the tendons, which pull on the bones to make them move.

Your **flexor tendons** are on the palms of your hands. Muscles in your arms pull on them to make your fingers *bend*.

Try this: Hold one hand palm-up and wiggle your fingers. With the other hand, touch the center of your wrist. Can you feel your **flexor tendons** moving?

Your **extensor tendons** are on the back of your hands. Muscles in your arms pull on them to make your fingers *straighten*.

Try this: Look at the back of one of your hands while you wiggle your fingers. You can see your **extensor tendons** moving as they pull on the bones of your hand.

Directions: Fill in the blanks.

① _____ attach bones to other bones at joints.

② _____ attach muscles to bones and pull to move the bones.

How Does It Work?

Activity: Make a Working Hand Model

Materials

- ☐ cardstock
- ☐ pencil
- ☐ scissors
- ☐ straws
- ☐ tape
- ☐ yarn

Directions

1. Trace around your hand on cardstock paper. Cut out your hand shape.

2. Draw a line to mark each joint on the fingers and thumbs. If your paper is very thick, you may want to pre-bend each joint.

3. Cut straws and tape them onto the hand as shown in the diagram.

   > Use three straws for each finger and two straws for the thumb.

   > Leave a small gap between the straws at the joints so they can move.

4. Thread yarn through the straws as shown in the diagram. Tape the yarn down at the fingertips so it doesn't pull out through the straws.

5. Pull on the yarn to bend the fingers. The strings are like the flexor tendons in your hands, pulling to bend your fingers.

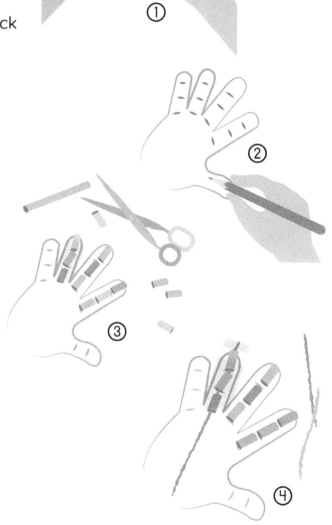

Tip: Wrap tape around the end of the yarn to create a "needle" to make threading easier.

600 Muscles

It is true! You have about 600 muscles in your body. They are all made of stretchy tissue, like rubber bands. Each muscle is made of thousands of these long, stretchy **fibers** all bundled together.

Muscles can **contract**, or squeeze together. When they relax, they go back to their original size. *This means that muscles can pull, but they cannot push.*

Exercise doesn't give you more **muscle fibers**, but it makes the muscles you have **bigger**.

TRY THIS!

Hold a rubber band with one hand and pull on it with the other hand to stretch it out. You can **pull** a rubber band, but can you **push** it?

Three Kinds of Muscles

You have three kinds of muscles:

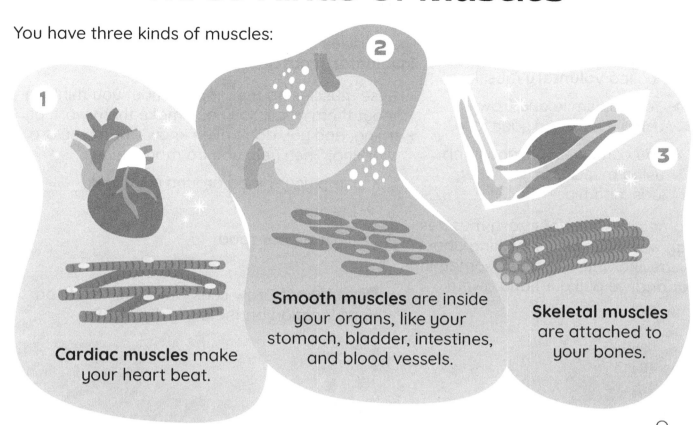

Cardiac muscles make your heart beat.

Smooth muscles are inside your organs, like your stomach, bladder, intestines, and blood vessels.

Skeletal muscles are attached to your bones.

Did you know...

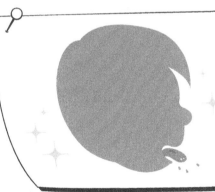

Your **tongue** is made up of 8 muscles working together. It is the only skeletal muscle in your body that is attached only at one end. AND it doesn't get tired like other muscles!

Can your tongue do tricks?

Can you curl your tongue?

Can you flip or fold your tongue?

Can you make a clover? Not everyone can!

Are You in Control?

The muscles you can control are called **voluntary** muscles.

➤ You can smile and frown using muscles in your face.

➤ You can walk, run, and jump using muscles in your feet, legs, and hips.

Sometimes our **voluntary muscles** can work without us thinking about them, like when we touch something hot and we pull our hand away.

The muscles that you cannot control are called **involuntary muscles**.

These muscles do their jobs without you thinking about them at all. You can't make them work by trying, and you don't even know when they are working! They help you do many things:

➤ pump your blood around your body

➤ breathe

➤ digest your food

Directions: Draw lines from each body part to its location on the body diagram.

Voluntary Muscles

face

arm

leg

Involuntary Muscles

heart

stomach

intestines

Directions: Circle whether you would use **voluntary** or **involuntary** muscles.

Digesting your lunch	voluntary	involuntary
Kicking a ball	voluntary	involuntary
Moving blood around your body	voluntary	involuntary
Smiling	voluntary	involuntary

Muscle Facts

Muscles in your lips, tongue, cheeks, throat, and jaw are just some of the muscles that work together to help you speak!

It takes more muscles to frown than it does to smile. Draw a smile.

Only humans can pinch each finger to their thumb one at a time. Try to do it with each hand.

There are no muscles in your fingers, thumbs, or toes! Tendons do the work.

Your *hardest-working* muscle is your heart. It never stops pumping!

Surprise! Your strongest muscle is your **masseter**, which closes your jaw. Humans have a powerful bite!

Your *largest* muscle is your **gluteus maximus**. You sit on it!

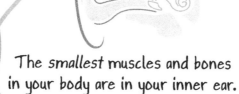

The *smallest* muscles and bones in your body are in your inner ear. They help you hear.

Your *fastest* moving muscles are your eye muscles.

Draw and write about your favorite way to use your muscles.

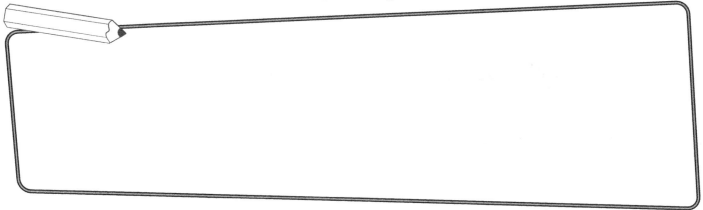

Your Nervous System

Your nervous system controls everything you do, including *moving*, *breathing*, *thinking*, *remembering*, and *feeling*. Try these activities:

☐ Blink your eyes.

☐ Take a deep breath.

☐ Think of your favorite animal.

☐ Remember a time when you felt warm.

Now, thank your **nervous system** for allowing you to do these things!

Directions: Color the brain and spinal cord (central nervous system) green. Color the nerves in the diagram blue.

Your **brain** controls your body. It is like a computer, only much faster and more powerful and complex. It looks like a gray, wrinkly lump and will weigh about 3 pounds when you are an adult.

Your **spinal cord** runs from your brain down your back through your spine. It carries messages back and forth from your brain to other parts of your body.

Nerves carry messages from your central nervous system to all parts of your body. You have so many nerves that we couldn't draw them all here!

HERE'S A VISUAL!
Make your hands into fists.
Hold your two fists together.
That is about the size of your brain.

WOW!
There are over **7 trillion** nerves in your body!
Fill in all the zeros to write 7 trillion:

7,___ ___ ___ ,___ ___ ___ ,___ ___ ___ ,___ ___ ___

Your Body's Boss

Your **brain** is the boss of your body. It controls **everything** you do. It keeps your heart beating and warns you when there is trouble. Without your brain, you couldn't survive, and you wouldn't be you!

Parts of Your Brain

Working Together

Your **brain** needs blood flow for food and oxygen.

Arteries bring fresh blood into your brain.

Veins take waste out.

The **cerebrum** is the outside part of your brain. It's where lots of conscious things happen, like *thinking, moving,* and *sensing.*

You *learn* and *remember* by forming connections in this part of the brain.

The **cerebellum** is under the cerebrum. It helps you *move* and *keep your balance.*

At the bottom of your brain is the **medulla.** It is also called the **brain stem.** It *connects your brain to your spinal cord.*

The medulla does the important things you don't think about like your *heartbeat* and *breathing.*

Directions: Use the color code to color the brain and write two things each part does.

Cerebrum—green _____ _____

Medulla—red _____ _____

Cerebellum—blue _____ _____

The different regions of the brain also form connections with each other. For example, when you learn how to ride a bike you are forming connections between your **cerebrum** (thinking) and your **cerebellum** (moving and balance).

What's in All Those Wrinkles?

The **cerebrum** is the biggest part of your brain. It is the wrinkly part around the outside. Different parts of your cerebrum do different things.

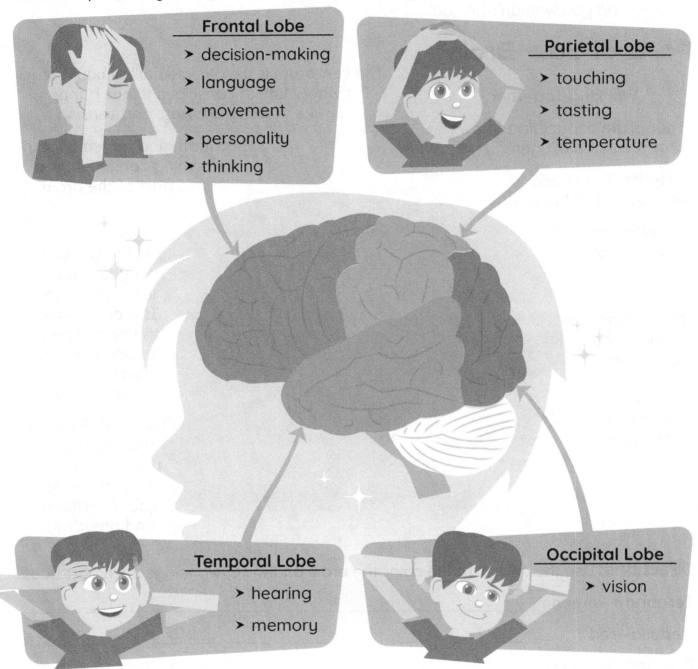

Frontal Lobe
> decision-making
> language
> movement
> personality
> thinking

Parietal Lobe
> touching
> tasting
> temperature

Temporal Lobe
> hearing
> memory

Occipital Lobe
> vision

Directions: Use your hands to show where the different lobes of your brain are and state what each part does.

Did you know that parts of the cerebrum can get bigger if you use them a lot? Musicians tend to have larger temporal lobes.

42

Fun Facts About Your Amazing Brain

Your brain sends more messages each day than ALL of the messages sent by cell phones in the world. There are about **86,000,000,000 neurons**, or nerve cells, in your brain.

Synapses are the places where communication between cells happens. There are more synapses in your brain than there are stars in the Milky Way!

Your brain is about **60%** fat, the most of any organ in your body.

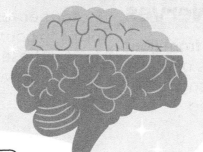

The right side of your brain controls the left side of your body and vice versa.

20% of the energy you get from food is used by your brain, even though your brain is only about **2%** of your body weight.

Your Wrinkly Brain

Materials

☐ 2 sheets of paper

Directions

1. Crumple up a sheet of paper into a ball.

2. Set the crumpled-up sheet of paper on a flat piece of paper.

3. Compare the two sheets of paper.

   Do they have the same surface area?   **yes no**

   Could they both fit into the same space?   **yes no**

Does it make more sense now?

Your brain is wrinkly like the crumpled-up ball of paper. This allows more brain to fit inside your skull. If you smoothed all the wrinkles out of your brain and made it flat, it would be about the size of a small tablecloth.

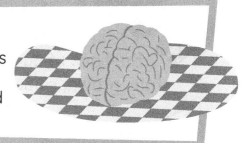

     #8386 My Body Is Amazing

Passing Messages

How does your nervous system send messages to the rest of your body?

Neurons are special cells that can pass messages to each other. But they only carry messages in one direction. In your brain, neurons connect to each other like a very complicated spiderweb with each neuron connecting to many others.

Nerves are mostly made of neurons connected in chains or webs, moving messages around your body where they need to go.

Sensory and Motor Nerves

Sensory nerves carry messages from your eyes, ears, skin, and other parts of your body to your brain. These messages tell your brain what you are sensing.

Motor nerves carry messages from your brain to your muscles and other body parts. These messages tell your body how to move or react.

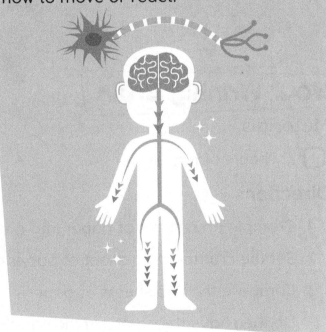

WOW! The **sciatic nerves** are the largest nerves in your body. They run from your lower spine down the back of each leg and into your feet. When you are fully grown, some of the neurons in your sciatic nerves will be **3** feet long!

44

Your Nervous System in Action

What has to happen for you to catch a ball? Here's how your nervous system can work.

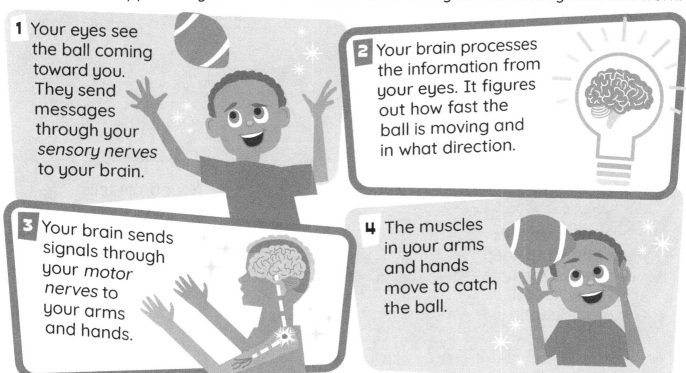

1 Your eyes see the ball coming toward you. They send messages through your *sensory nerves* to your brain.

2 Your brain processes the information from your eyes. It figures out how fast the ball is moving and in what direction.

3 Your brain sends signals through your *motor nerves* to your arms and hands.

4 The muscles in your arms and hands move to catch the ball.

This sounds simple, but it is not! Any movement, like *catching a ball*, *walking*, *chewing*, or *even scratching an itch* can involve many different nerves sending and receiving many messages to and from the brain.

How speedy is your nervous system?

Materials ☐ a partner ☐ a ruler

Directions

1. Hold a ruler out in front of you.

2. Have your partner hold their hand near the bottom of the ruler, ready to catch it.

3. Let go of the ruler. Did your partner catch it? Try it a few more times.

4. Switch places and try to catch the ruler yourself.

5. Take turns and see how close to the bottom of the ruler you can catch it.

What's going on?

It happens very quickly! Your eyes see the ruler start to move. They send a message to your brain. Your brain sends a message to your muscles to close your fingers and catch the ruler.

Autonomic Nerves Are Automatic!

Autonomic nerves are special kinds of motor nerves that carry messages from your brain to your organs. You don't even know they are doing it!

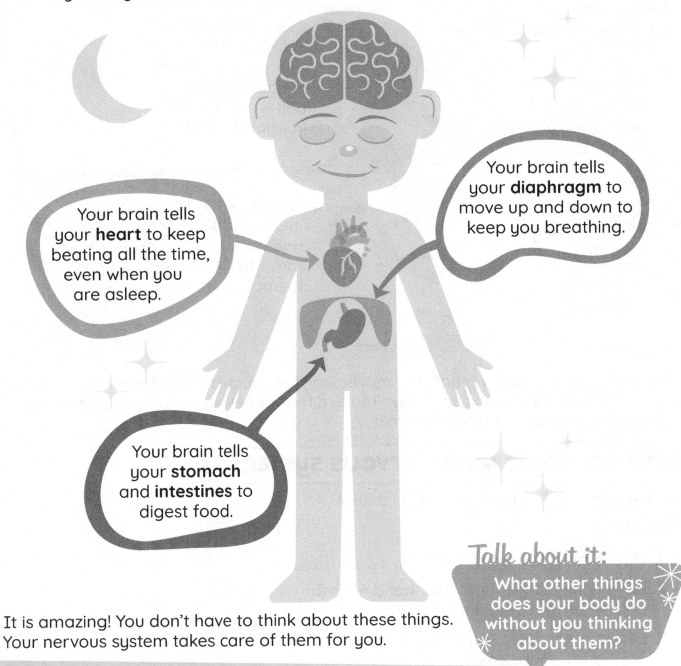

Your brain tells your **heart** to keep beating all the time, even when you are asleep.

Your brain tells your **diaphragm** to move up and down to keep you breathing.

Your brain tells your **stomach** and **intestines** to digest food.

It is amazing! You don't have to think about these things. Your nervous system takes care of them for you.

Talk about it: What other things does your body do without you thinking about them?

Directions: Complete each statement.

1 Your brain sends messages to your heart to _____.

2 Your brain tells your diaphragm to _____.

3 Your brain tells your stomach and intestines to _____.

46

Taking Control

Most of the time your nervous system keeps you breathing without you having to pay any attention. But if you want to, you can take control and breathe on purpose. This is also true of other movements like *blinking* and *swallowing*.

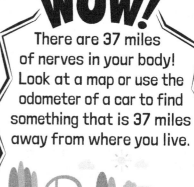

There are 37 miles of nerves in your body! Look at a map or use the odometer of a car to find something that is 37 miles away from where you live.

TRY THESE!

➤ Blink your eyes three times.

➤ Take a little breath and breathe out.

➤ Take a deep breath and blow it all out.

See, some things can be both *automatic* and *on purpose*.

Now, let's take control! Name some scenarios when you might do the following things on purpose:

Blink: _____

_____

Hold your breath: _____

Exhale (blow out) a deep breath: _____

Swallow: _____

Directions: Draw or write about something that your body does that can be both *automatic* and *on purpose*.

Act Fast!

Your nervous system has some built-in reactions called **reflexes**. Reflexes are **involuntary**, which means they happen without you thinking about them. Have you ever been so scared that you jumped or screamed? Those reactions are reflexes, and so are these:

✓ sneezing ✓ coughing ✓ blinking ✓ flinching ✓ gagging ✓ pupils changing size

Here's how a reflex works:

1 You touch something *prickly*.

2 The sensory receptors in your fingers send a message to your nervous system.

3 The message travels to your spinal cord.

4 Your spinal cord sends a message right back through your arm to your hand.

The Message: Pull your hand away!

Reflexes happen very quickly because they are meant to keep your body safe. The message is so important that it doesn't need to go all the way to your brain to get a response!

Test Your Reflexes

Materials   ☐ a partner   ☐ a window or screen   ☐ some cotton balls

Directions

1. Have your partner stand on the other side of a window.

2. Toss a cotton ball at the window near their face.

3. Watch for their reflexes. Do they blink or flinch?

4. Trade places, and have your partner test your reflexes.

What did you do? _____

How do reflexes keep you safe? _____

_____

The Big 5

How do you know what your pillow feels like? Or what art looks like? Or what your favorite song sounds like? Your **senses** tell you all about the world around you.

Directions: Fill in the blanks to show which senses are used by certain parts of the body.

Word Bank
hearing   touch   smell   taste   sight

Directions: Draw something you would use each sense to explore.

hearing	touch	smell	taste	sight

How Do Your Senses Work?

Your body has **sensory receptor cells** that take in information from the outside world. For example, your eyes have sensory cells that detect light. These cells turn the information about light into electrical signals that travel to your brain. Your brain interprets the information so you can understand it.

Directions: Draw a line to match each sensory organ to the kind of information it senses.

① **eyes**

② **ears**

③ **nose**

④ **tongue**

⑤ **skin**

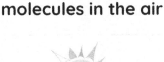

molecules in the air

light

sound waves

surface textures

chemicals in food

WOW! Some people's brains experience senses differently than other people's brains. *Synesthesia* is when a person experiences one sense through another. For example, they might see music as colors. Or they could sense numbers as tastes.

Your Eyes Are Amazing!

Your **eyeballs** are like balls of jelly. Your **eyelids** protect your eyeballs and keep them from drying out.

Directions: Read the information below and finish writing the name of each part to label the diagram.

The colored part of your eye is called the **iris**. The black part inside the iris is the **pupil**. The iris can make the pupil bigger and smaller to control the amount of light that goes into your eyes.

Try this: Have a friend close their eyes and count to ten. Watch closely when they open their eyes. You will see their pupils change size!

A **retina** is at the back of each eye. Light comes in through the cornea and pupil, is focused by the lens, and hits your retina. Special cells on your retina called *photoreceptors* send electrical signals to your brain through your **optic nerve**. Your brain translates the signals into a picture.

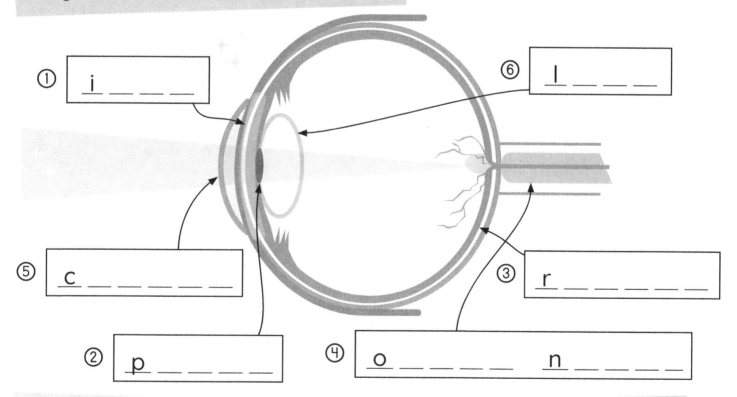

① i _ _ _

⑥ l _ _ _

⑤ c _ _ _ _ _ _

③ r _ _ _ _ _ _

② p _ _ _ _ _

④ o _ _ _ _ _ n _ _ _ _ _

Your **cornea** is like a clear window at the front of your eyeball. It helps focus the light coming into your eye. It also protects your iris and pupil.

Behind your pupil is your **lens**. It focuses light as it comes in through your pupil. It helps you focus on things whether they are close to you or far away.

Try this: Look closely at your hand. Then, look across the room. Your lens just changed shape to change your focus!

Light Sensors

Your **retinas** have two kinds of **photoreceptor cells** that sense light. They are called **cones** and **rods**. The cone cells and rod cells in your retina turn information about light into electrical signals. They send these signals through the **optic nerve** to your brain.

Directions: Color the cones red, green, and blue. One color will be repeated.

CONES

Cones sense *red, blue,* and *green*. Your amazing brain combines signals from these 3 colors to see *millions* of colors. If some of your cone cells don't work, you can be **color blind**.

You have about 7 million cones in each eye.

Cones need a lot of light to work.

You can't see colors in the dark!

RODS

Rods sense black, white, and gray.

You have about 120 million rods in each eye.

Rods work day and night.

Rods tell you about the shape and movement of things.

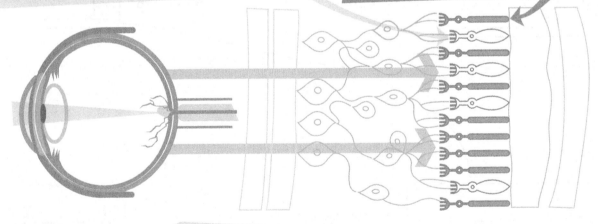

WOW!

The image on your **retina** is upside down! Your brain translates it to right-side up.

TRY THIS!

Grab a big, shiny spoon. Look at your reflection in the bowl of the spoon. What do you see? This is a bit like the image on your retina.

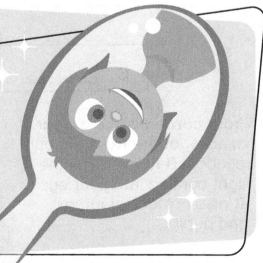

Fooling Your Eyes and Your Brain

Your eyes are great at helping you see the world around you, but they are not perfect. Scientists sometimes use **optical illusions** to learn about how our eyes and brain work.

Depth Perception

Why do you have two eyes? Each eye sees from a slightly different angle.

1. Close one eye and look at something small far away.

2. Hold up your thumb to cover the object.

3. Hold your thumb still and switch eyes. What happens?

What is going on?
Each eye takes in the object from a different angle. Your brain merges the two images together to tell how far away things are. This gives us **depth perception**—the ability to tell how *near* or *far* something is.

Floating Finger Illusion

1. Point your index fingers toward each other, almost touching. Hold them a few inches in front of your eyes.

2. Focus your eyes on the opposite side of the room.

3. Do you see the floating finger with two fingernail ends?　　**yes**　　**no**

4. Slowly move your fingers closer and farther apart.

What happens? _____

What is going on? Each of your eyes sees your fingers from a different angle. Your brain tries to make sense of the conflicting images and comes up with a floating, double-ended finger.

Peripheral Vision

Try this: Hold your hands near the sides of your head. Look straight ahead. Slowly move your hands backwards until you can't see them anymore.

This is how far you can see to the side using your **peripheral vision**.

Twelve Black Dots Illusion

Can you see all 12 black dots on this grid of gray lines at the same time?

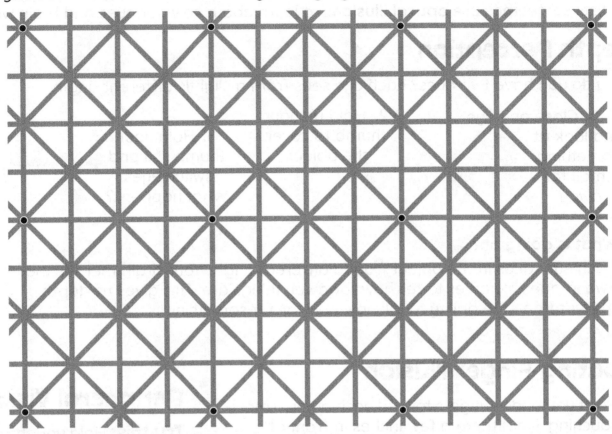

What's going on?

Yes, there are really 12 black dots! You only see a dot or two when they are in the center of your vision. But your peripheral vision can't see them unless you move your eyes! Your brain predicts that there will just be more intersecting gray lines, so you don't see the black dots.

YOUR BLIND SPOT

Your retina has a blind spot—it's an area that can't sense anything. This is where your optic nerve connects to your retina.

Try this: Hold this page about 20 inches in front of you. Close your right eye. Focus your left eye on the **+** and slowly move the page towards you until the dot disappears.

There's your blind spot! You can move the page closer and farther away and watch the dot reappear and disappear.

Ready for More Illusions?

Arrows Illusion

Directions: Look at the horizontal lines. Are they the same length, or is one longer than the other?

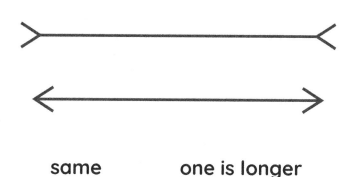

same   one is longer

Scientists aren't sure why most people's brains see the top line as longer, but they are actually the same length! Check by holding a ruler or the edge of a piece of paper over the ends of the lines.

Shades of Gray

Directions: Look at the two square boxes in the rectangles.

Which one is darker, or are they the same?   A   B   same

A   B

This is known as the *contrast illusion*. Our brain compares the brightness of things that are next to each other. The greater the difference between light and dark, the brighter the light-colored object will seem. The center boxes are actually the same color!

C

What can you do to prove that the gray bar in **C** is actually one color?

_____

_____

_____

How Do You Sense Taste?

For starters, there are about **10,000 taste buds** on your tongue! There are more taste buds at the back than on the sides or front of your tongue. These tiny organs sense different flavors and send messages to your brain about what is in your mouth. Your taste buds taste five different tastes.

Directions: Draw or write your favorite food in each flavor group.

Tasty Test

Materials ☐ paper towels   ☐ salt or sugar   ☐ water

1. Dry your tongue off with a clean paper towel.

2. Sprinkle a little bit of salt or sugar on your dry tongue. Can you taste it?

3. Take a sip of water to moisten your tongue and repeat the test.

4. This time, move the salt or sugar around your mouth to mix it with saliva.

Look at your tongue in a mirror. The tiny red bumps you see are **papillae** (puh-PILL-ee). Each papilla has taste buds inside it.

Did you get a different sensation this time? Explain. _____

What's going on?

Your teeth and **saliva** help you taste. Your taste buds cannot sense chunks of food. They need tiny bits that are mixed into your saliva. (Saliva is spit!) So, chew your food well to enjoy your favorite tastes.

Taste Bud Facts

Taste buds only live about 10 days. They are constantly replaced by new ones. Your body makes new taste buds every two weeks or so.

You lose taste buds as you get older. Older people have about 5,000 taste buds.

"Hot" and "spicy" are not tastes. They are sensations of heat sent by pain receptors.

The back of your tongue is especially good at sensing bitterness. This can help you detect and spit out poisonous foods!

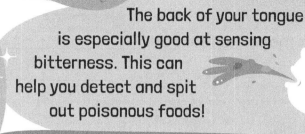

Did you know...Your brain makes things taste better when you are hungry!

BIG QUESTION! If your tongue can only taste five different kinds of tastes, how can our sense of taste detect about **100,000** different flavors?

Team Up #1

Your sense of taste comes from both your mouth and your nose!

It starts when you smell something delicious by inhaling air molecules through your nose. But it doesn't stop there!

Your brain puts together the information from your taste buds and from your nose to make each flavor you taste.

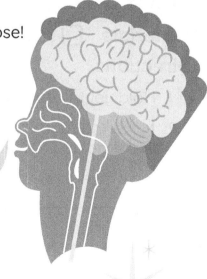

| Taste buds | + | Nose | → | Flavor |

Team Up #2

Your tongue and your teeth team up, too!

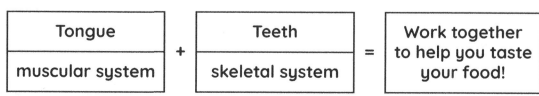

Tongue		Teeth		Work together
--------	---	-------	---	to help you taste
muscular system	+	skeletal system	=	your food!

The Team Up

Smell and taste are both linked to your **autonomic nervous system**. Strong flavors can make you gag, and wonderful tastes and smells can make you feel good.

Smells that make me feel good. _____

_____

Smells that make me feel bad. _____

_____

Tastes I enjoy. _____

_____

Tastes I do not like. _____

_____

Try It Solo

Materials ☐ 3 tasty foods

Directions

1. Hold your breath and put a bit of food in your mouth.

2. Move the food around your tongue. Don't breathe in yet! What do you taste?

3. Now take a few slow breaths through your nose while the food is in your mouth.

4. Write the name of each food and circle whether there was a difference *with* or *without* breaths.

Foods Tasted	Differences	
Food 1:	Yes	No
Food 2:	Yes	No
Food 3:	Yes	No

One Trillion Scents!

WOW!

Most humans can identify more than 1 trillion scents!
Write 12 zeros to make the number 1 trillion:

1,___ ___ ___,___ ___ ___,___ ___ ___,___ ___ ___

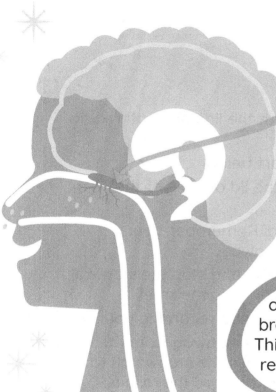

High up inside your nose are cells that sense smells. They take in information from the tiny particles in the air and send messages to the **olfactory bulb** in your brain.

This is where your brain makes sense of information it gets about the smells you can taste and smells you cannot taste, like flowers, soap, and puppy breath!

The olfactory bulb is directly connected to the parts of your brain that handle memories and emotions. This is why certain smells can make you remember something or feel a certain way.

What smell reminds you of something?

The smell of _____

reminds me of _____ .

Draw it here.

What smell makes you feel a certain way?

The smell of _____

makes me feel _____ .

Draw it here.

Smells Travel Through the Air

Activity: The Smell Test

Materials

☐ 4 smelly substances, such as a teaspoon of vinegar, a few drops of perfume, a teaspoon of vanilla extract, lemon or orange peels, chopped garlic, or flowers

☐ 4 small containers with tight-fitting lids

☐ a stopwatch

☐ a partner

Directions

1. Put one smelly substance in each container. Put the lids on tightly so no smell escapes.

2. Write the names of each substance in the chart below.

3. Once you are ready, have your partner take the lid off one of the containers and hold it **1 foot away** from you.

   Then, start the stopwatch as you start sniffing. Remember, your partner should be holding the container 1 foot away.

4. As soon as you can tell what the smell is, name it, and stop the stopwatch. Write down the amount of time it took you to identify the smell.

5. Do the same test with the other smells and continue recording your results.

6. Repeat the tests, but this time move at least **10 feet away** from the containers. Have your partner open each container as you use the stopwatch to measure how long it takes you to identify each smell, and record the results.

Substance Tested	Time at 1 Foot	Time at 10 Feet

What's going on?

The small smell particles in each substance have to travel through the air, into your nose, and to your brain before you can smell them.

Compare the times it took to smell each item. _____

What's That Sound?

TRY THIS! Sit still and listen. What do you hear?

Your sense of hearing takes in *loud* sounds, *quiet* sounds, *high-pitched* sounds, and *low-pitched* sounds. Think of a dog barking or wind rustling through the trees.

Draw what you heard.

How Do We Hear?

1. Sound happens when something moves or *vibrates*. Hearing happens when the sound vibrations travel through the air to your ears.

2. Your **pinna** and **ear canal** make up your **outer ear**. They funnel sound waves into your ear.

3. Your **eardrum** is in your **middle ear**. It is thin skin stretched tight like the head of a drum. Sound waves make your eardrum *vibrate*, or move back and forth, very quickly.

4. The vibration of your eardrum moves the tiny bones (**ossicles**) in your middle ear.

5. The vibration goes into your fluid-filled, snail-shaped **cochlea**.

6. Your cochlea sends electrical signals along your **auditory nerve** to your brain.

Directions: Label the **inner ear, middle ear**, and **outer ear** on the lines below the diagram.

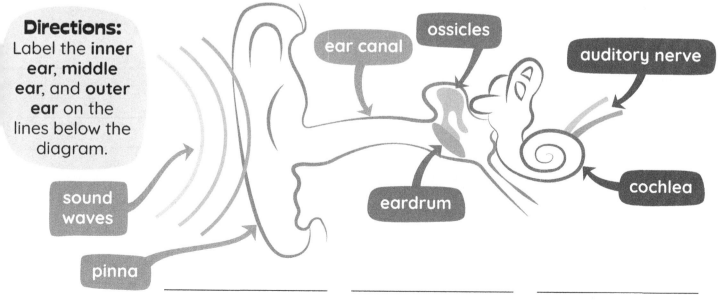

ear canal   ossicles   auditory nerve   sound waves   eardrum   cochlea   pinna

_____   _____   _____

How Does Your Eardrum Work?

Make an Eardrum Model

Materials

- ☐ a bowl
- ☐ plastic wrap
- ☐ rubber band or tape
- ☐ I teaspoon salt

Directions

1. Stretch a layer of plastic wrap tightly over the bowl.

2. Secure the plastic wrap with a rubber band or tape.

3. Pull the plastic wrap to get all the wrinkles out.

   Note: The tighter and smoother the plastic wrap is, the better your eardrum model will work!

4. Sprinkle the salt on the plastic wrap. Spread it around so it's not in a pile.

5. Make some noise! Yell, clap your hands, bang pots and pans, or play loud music through a speaker near the bowl. Observe what happens to the salt.

Describe what the salt does. _____

_____

What's going on?

Your eardrum has skin stretched tightly across it, like the plastic wrap on your model. The sound waves (noise) you made vibrated the plastic wrap, which made the salt bounce around.

As sound waves enter your ear, they make your eardrum vibrate in much the same way.

Your Sense of Balance

Have you ever gotten dizzy or carsick? That means your **vestibular sense** is off! In other words, your brain is getting confused by conflicting signals from your vestibular system and your eyes.

What part of your body senses all of this for you? Your inner ear. This crazy structure in your inner ear looks kind of like an alien or a weird sea creature! It is called the **vestibular labyrinth**.

The fluid-filled canals (**loops**) and the part they are attached to are part of your **vestibular system**.

The **cochlea** is the part that looks like a snail shell. It is involved in hearing.

Directions: Fill a clear cup less than halfway with water. Without spilling the water, carefully tip the cup from front to back and side to side.

What's going on?

See how the water moves? That is how the fluid in your inner ear moves. The position of the fluid sends signals to your brain about how your head is moving. Your brain uses this information to keep you upright when you sit, stand, walk, run, and jump.

Test 1 Stand on one foot. Can you feel your muscles working to keep you from falling over?

What's happening? Your inner ear is sending signals to your brain, which sends signals to your muscles.

Test 2 Find an open space like a lawn or sandy area where you won't run into anything. Close your eyes and spin around 10–20 times. Then stop and open your eyes.

What's happening? As you spin around, the fluid inside your inner ear starts spinning around. When you stop moving, the fluid keeps moving! Your brain gets confusing signals, so you feel dizzy until the fluid in your ear settles down.

What Does a Cat's Fur Feel Like?

Or wind blowing on your face? Or a hug from someone who loves you? Your **somatosensory system** helps you feel things with your sense of touch.

Sensors

You have many different kinds of sensors in your skin, joints, and muscles. They can take in information about things touching you, but also about temperature, movement, and pain. These different receptors send messages to your brain, which puts them all together to tell you what you are feeling.

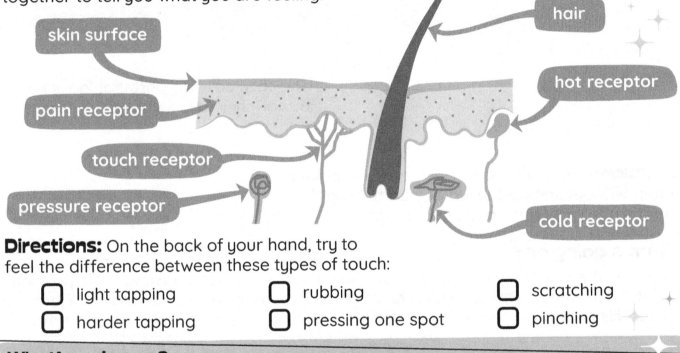

skin surface

hair

pain receptor

hot receptor

touch receptor

pressure receptor

cold receptor

Directions: On the back of your hand, try to feel the difference between these types of touch:

☐ light tapping   ☐ rubbing   ☐ scratching

☐ harder tapping   ☐ pressing one spot   ☐ pinching

What's going on?

Different kinds of **touch receptors** are sending information to your brain so you can tell the difference between different kinds of touch. These **sensors** take in information about the *pressure*, *location*, and *movement* of anything touching your skin.

Your Brain Makes Choices for You

Can you feel your clothes touching your skin? If you could feel everything all of the time, it would be overwhelming! So, your brain ignores signals that it has been receiving for a little while. It pays more attention to new or different signals.

Some areas of your body have more touch receptors than others.

➤ You have the **most** touch receptors in your *fingers, toes, mouth,* and *lips.*

➤ The **least** sensitive part of you is the *middle of your back.* That area has few touch receptors.

Can You Feel Two?

Touch Test

Materials ☐ 2 toothpicks ☐ a partner ☐ *optional:* a blindfold

Directions

1. Have your partner hold out one arm and close their eyes. Explain that you are going to touch their forearm gently with the toothpicks. Their job is to tell you if you touched them with *one* or *two* toothpicks.

2. Gently touch their forearm with the two toothpicks very close together— almost touching each other. **You need to touch both toothpicks to their skin at exactly the same time.**

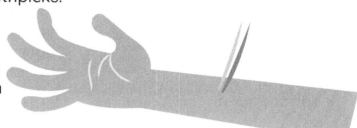

3. Ask your partner if you touched them with one or two toothpicks.

4. Now touch very gently with two toothpicks about half an inch apart. Continue the test with the toothpicks a little farther apart each time. Keep doing it until your partner can feel both toothpicks.

5. Do the same test on your friend's fingertip, starting with the toothpicks almost touching each other and moving them a tiny bit farther apart each time you touch.

   Is there a difference in your friend's answers from when you touched their forearm?   **yes**   **no**

   Explain: _____

   _____

6. Switch roles and have your partner try this test on you.

7. Try this test on the skin from different areas of your body like your *cheek, foot, shoulder, back, lip*, or *knee* to see which areas have more or fewer touch sensors.

WOW!

Your fingertips have about **100** times more touch sensors per square inch than the skin on your back!

What's going on?

The **touch sensors** in your *forearm* are spread out. It feels like there is only one toothpick touching you when the toothpicks are close enough together to be felt by just one sensor. They have to be far enough apart to be sensed by two sensors for you to feel both of them (about 2 inches on the forearm).

Your *fingertips* have many more touch sensors per square inch than your forearm, so you can feel both toothpicks even when they are close together.

Proprioception

Big word alert! Say, **pro-pree-o-SEP-shun!**

Proprioception is your sense of body awareness. It helps you know where your body parts are without looking at them. It's what lets you run up the stairs without looking at each step or throw a ball without watching your arm and hand.

Sensory receptors in your joints and muscles give you information about where your body is and how it is moving.

Try this: Close your eyes and touch your finger to your nose. That's **proprioception!**

Now try this: Hold one hand high above your head and close your eyes. With the other hand, touch the index finger of the hand over your head.

Did you get it on the first try? If not, try it again. Your sense of proprioception is telling you where your hands are and how they relate to each other.

Like your sense of sight, your **sense of proprioception** isn't perfect. It can be fooled!

The Dead Finger Illusion

Materials ☐ a partner

Directions

1. Hold your hand up against your friend's hand, like you are giving a high five.

2. With your other hand, place your thumb and index finger on either side of you and your partner's index fingers (see diagram).

3. Move your fingers up and down along the index fingers. What do you feel?

What's going on?

The information going to your brain from one hand says you are touching your index finger on both sides, so that is what your brain expects. When it receives information from just the back of the index finger, it interprets that as your finger being numb.

Hot or Cold? Your Skin Sensors Know!

Your skin has sensors that tell you about temperature. If you touch an ice cube, the sensors send messages to your brain telling you they feel *cold*. When the sun shines on your skin in the summer, sensors send messages to your brain telling you they feel *hot*.

Warm or Cold?

Materials

☐ 3 jars or bowls of water: I cold, I warm (not hot), I room temperature

☐ towel or paper towels

Directions

1. Put one hand in the bowl of cold water and the other hand in the bowl of warm water and count to 20.

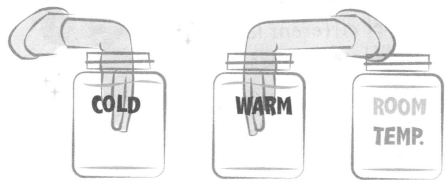

2. Then, put both hands in the room temperature bowl of water.

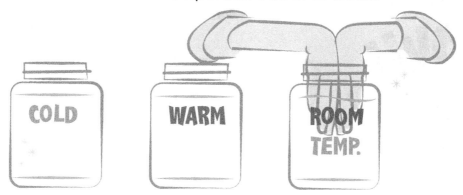

3. What do you feel? _____

_____

What's going on?

Your temperature sensory receptors don't tell you the exact temperature of what you are touching. They just tell your brain the difference between what you are touching now and what you touched before!

Pain Is Not Fun!

So why do we feel pain? Pain helps to keep us safe and healthy.

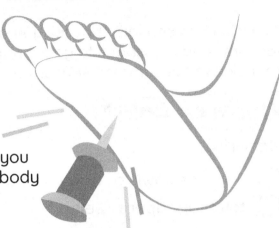

➤ A *sharp pain* causes your nervous system to quickly move your body away from what is hurting it.

➤ A *dull pain*, such as an ache in your leg, keeps you from moving or using the injured part of your body so it can heal over time.

Did you know...

People experience pain differently, and you can feel different levels of pain at different times.

If you are in a good mood ☺ and stub your toe, it will hurt, but if you are in a bad mood ☹ and stub your toe, it will hurt more!

WOW!

You have over **3 million** pain receptors in your body, but you have **no pain receptors** in your *hair, nails,* or *brain*!

Just like other sense receptors, **pain receptors** are not evenly distributed over your body.

Directions

Pinch the skin on your elbow. Then pinch yourself on the inside of your arm, just above the elbow.

Which hurts more?   **forearm   elbow**

What's going on?

Pain signals from your body go to lots of different places in the brain, including the part that handles *emotion*. How you are feeling can affect how your brain pays attention to the pain signals.

Food to Fuel

What happens to food when you eat it? Your **digestive system** breaks your food down into very small pieces so that your body can use it.

esophagus

mouth

Why Do You Eat?

Food powers your body!

Food gives you energy to live and to move.

Food provides the "building blocks" that your cells use to repair themselves and to make more cells.

liver

stomach

gallbladder

pancreas

small intestine

large intestine

WOW! You will eat about **55** tons of food in your lifetime. That's about the weight of **8** elephants!

55 TONS

Draw your favorite food.

Does your favorite food make your mouth water when you smell it?

yes   **no**

Is it chewy, crispy, juicy or something else?

_____

The Digestive Process

Directions: Draw a line from each step of the digestive system to the part of the body where it happens. Then, trace the path of your food through the digestive system.

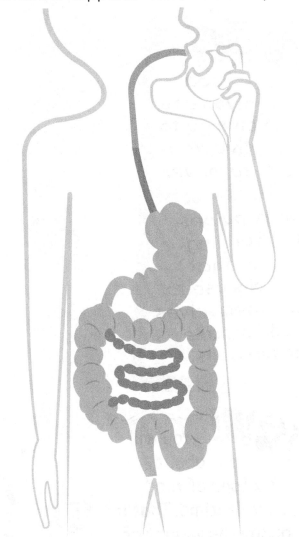

Chew and Mix: You put food in your **mouth** and chew it into smaller pieces. Food mixes with **saliva** to make it softer.

Swallow and Push: You swallow the mushy food. It moves down your **esophagus**, a muscular tube that pushes food toward your stomach.

Squeeze, Squish, and Squirt: Your **stomach** squeezes and squishes the food into a soupy mixture called **chyme** (kime). Then, it squirts acid into the chyme to break the food down into smaller particles.

Add, Break Down, and Move: Chyme goes into your **small intestine**. Chemicals called **enzymes** are added from your gallbladder and pancreas to break food down even further.

Tiny particles that your body needs move out of your small intestine and into your bloodstream.

Exit: Leftover material is formed into *feces* in your **large intestine**. (Feces is poop!) Feces exit the body.

Directions: Match each word to its definition.

Chyme	Enzymes	Saliva

① _____ are chemicals in the small intestine used to break food down.

② _____ is a soupy food mixture created in the stomach.

③ _____ is a mixture of water and chemicals, also called *spit*.

Chew, Mix, and Swallow

The first stop on food's journey through your digestive system is your mouth. Your **teeth**, **tongue**, and **saliva** are the beginning of digestion.

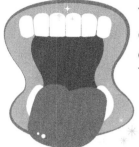

You may not think chewing your food is important, but it is! Your **teeth** cut and grind your food into smaller pieces that you can swallow. You don't want to choke because you swallowed too big a piece of food. The smaller the pieces, the easier they are to digest.

Your **tongue** not only helps you taste your food, it helps the food mix with **saliva** and moves it around your mouth as you chew.

About Your Teeth

Directions: Use the bold words to help you label the tooth.

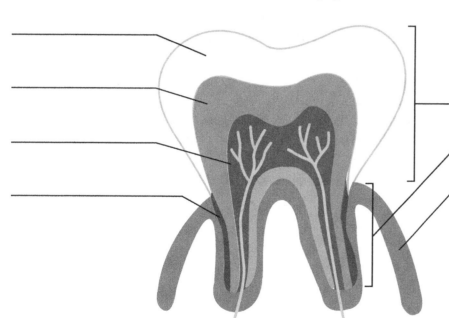

WOW! Your tooth enamel is the **hardest** part of your body!

Enamel covers the **crown**, or top part, of each tooth. It is harder than bone and protects your teeth from wear and tear.

Dentin is a thick layer under the enamel, which is sort of like bone. It is not quite as hard as the enamel.

Cementum covers the **roots** of teeth and helps them stick to the **bone** and stay in place in the **gums**.

Pulp is in the middle of the tooth. It is soft and contains nerves and blood vessels.

What is a tooth cavity?

A **cavity** is a hole in your enamel—the part you see! A dentist needs to fill in the hole so it won't get bigger.

The Right Tooth for the Job

Your teeth have four different shapes. Teeth are tools and you use each of them for different things.

Your **incisors** are right in the front.
They are shaped like chisels and have sharp edges.
These teeth can *bite* directly into foods like apples and sandwiches.

Your **canines** are next to your incisors.
They are pointy for *tearing* small pieces off of larger foods.
These teeth can tear off a tough piece of jerky or dried fruit.

Your **premolars** and **molars** are in the back of your mouth.
Molars are flat with ridges to crush and grind food.
These teeth are used for *chewing* foods like nuts, carrots, and gum.

How do you bite and chew?

Directions: Over the next day or so, pay attention to how you bite and chew different foods. In the chart below, write which foods you bite into or chew with each type of tooth.

Type of Tooth	Foods
Incisors	
Canines	
Premolars and Molars	

Two Sets of Teeth

Usually, babies are born without teeth so they can't chew food. Luckily, **20 teeth** come in during the first couple of years. As you get older, your "baby" teeth fall out and new, permanent teeth will take their place. Have you lost a tooth and grown a new one?

You will have **32 permanent teeth** when you are an adult. Your second set of teeth have to last for the rest of your life, so always brush and floss!

Directions: In the first picture, circle any teeth you have lost. In the second picture, circle the new teeth that have grown in.

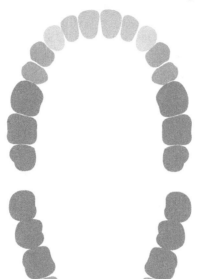

Do the Math

How many more adult teeth will you have than baby teeth?

_____ adult teeth

_____ baby teeth

_____ more adult teeth

You Need Spit!

Saliva, or spit, is mostly water with other chemicals mixed in. Saliva's main job is to wet the food in your mouth to help break it down. Spit comes from three pairs of **salivary glands** in your face and jaw.

Your salivary glands are always working to keep your mouth and throat moist. These glands make **extra** saliva when you eat. Once you swallow, it takes 7 to 10 seconds for food to get from your mouth to your stomach. It is pushed along by muscles in your **esophagus**.

TRY THIS!

Take a small sip of water and hold it in your mouth. Bend over and put your hands on the floor with your head upside down. Can you swallow while you are upside down?

yes   **no**

When you smell something delicious, your salivary glands get to work and make your mouth "water"!

Squeeze, Squish, and Squirt

Your **stomach** is a stretchy organ. It gets bigger when you eat, and can go from about the size of a tennis ball to as big as a soccer ball! It tells you when you are full. You also have a muscle that closes off the top of your stomach so food doesn't come back up. But if your body detects something in your stomach that can hurt you, such as bad bacteria, it will make the food come back up as vomit!

> Powerful muscles in your stomach **contract**, or squeeze, about three times each minute to squish up your food and break it into even smaller pieces.

> Your stomach also squirts *enzymes* and *acids* that dissolve the food into the soupy liquid called *chyme*. One of these acids is **hydrochloric acid**, which is strong enough to dissolve metal! It kills germs in food and helps break it down.

> Your stomach would digest itself if it didn't have a special **mucus** made by its inner lining to protect it.

> A meal usually spends about 4 hours in your stomach before it goes to the small intestine.

WOW!

Your stomach can secrete **2 liters** of gastric juices every day! This special liquid mixture includes *hydrochloric acid, water, electrolytes,* and *enzymes*.

Digestion Simulation

Materials

☐ soda crackers

☐ citrus juice (orange, lemon, or lime) or vinegar

☐ a plastic bag that seals well

Directions

1. Put a few crackers into a clear plastic bag and seal it well.

2. Squeeze the bag to break up the crackers into small pieces. This is like the muscles in your stomach contracting to squeeze your food and break it up. What does the food look like at this point?

3. Carefully open the bag and pour in some citrus juice. This is like the hydrochloric acid your stomach secretes (although not as strong).

4. Reseal the bag well and squeeze it some more. Your model stomach has made *chyme*, ready to go to the small intestine!

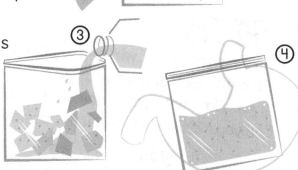

Gut Reactions

Directions: Read each callout below and then color each part of the digestive system.

Your **gallbladder** is a little green organ under your liver. It stores the bile made by your liver until your small intestine needs it to digest fats. **Color it green.**

Your **liver**, your largest internal organ, has about **500** jobs! It sorts out nutrients in your blood that come from your small intestine and much more. **Color it red.**

Your **stomach** turns food into *chyme*. **Color it orange.**

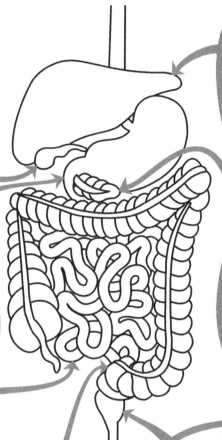

Your **pancreas** adds more enzymes to your small intestine to help with digestion. It also balances the sugar level in your body by releasing *insulin* into your blood. **Color it yellow.**

Nutrients are taken from the chyme in the **small intestine**. Most digestion occurs here. The nutrients move from the small intestine into your blood stream. It is called the "small" intestine because it is skinnier than your large intestine. **Color it blue.**

Leftover material is formed into *feces* and goes into the **rectum**. Then it leaves the body through the **anus**.

After the small intestine, what is left of your food goes into the **large intestine**. You have about **4 pounds** of good *bacteria* in your large intestine! These little critters get rid of *toxins* (poisons) and make vitamins your body needs. Healthy bacteria in your gut not only help keep you healthy, but scientists also think they can make you happier! **Color the large intestine purple.**

Did you know...

When gas is produced in your large intestine it is released as **flatulence** (farts!). Most people release gas at least **20 times** each day!

A mystery body part

Your **appendix** is a little tube attached to your large intestine. Scientists still aren't sure what the appendix does. It's a medical mystery!

Really! They Fit Where...?

Did you say 20 feet?

Materials

☐ 2 colors of yarn (*Color 1*—20 feet; *Color 2*—5 feet)

☐ a tape measure

☐ a bowl about the size of your abdomen

Directions

1. Measure out 20 feet of yarn (*Color 1*). Lay it out straight to see how long it is. This is *about* the length of your **small intestine**.

2. Measure out 5 feet of the other color yarn (*Color 2*). This is about the length of your **large intestine**.

3. Tie one end of the "small intestine" yarn to one end of the "large intestine" yarn.

4. Drop one end into the bowl and coil all of the yarn in after it. This is how your intestines fit in your abdomen.

large intestine

5 feet of yarn

small intestine

20 feet of yarn

Why do you think it is called the small intestine if it is longer? Discuss.

To Burp or Not to Burp?

You also swallow air while you are eating and drinking. Air is a gas! Often the gas comes back up as a **burp**, also known as a **belch**.

If you try to hold in a burp, it could make you uncomfortable since the air will now travel through your digestive system. And the "burp" will come out the other end...eventually!

Burping is a natural way to get rid of excess gas. Just remember to cover your mouth and say "excuse me."

Sometimes when we drink soda, we burp. That is because the bubbles in soda are carbon dioxide... a gas!

Put It All Together

Directions: Use the words and pictures on the left to help you to complete the statements about the digestive system. Read the statements when you are finished.

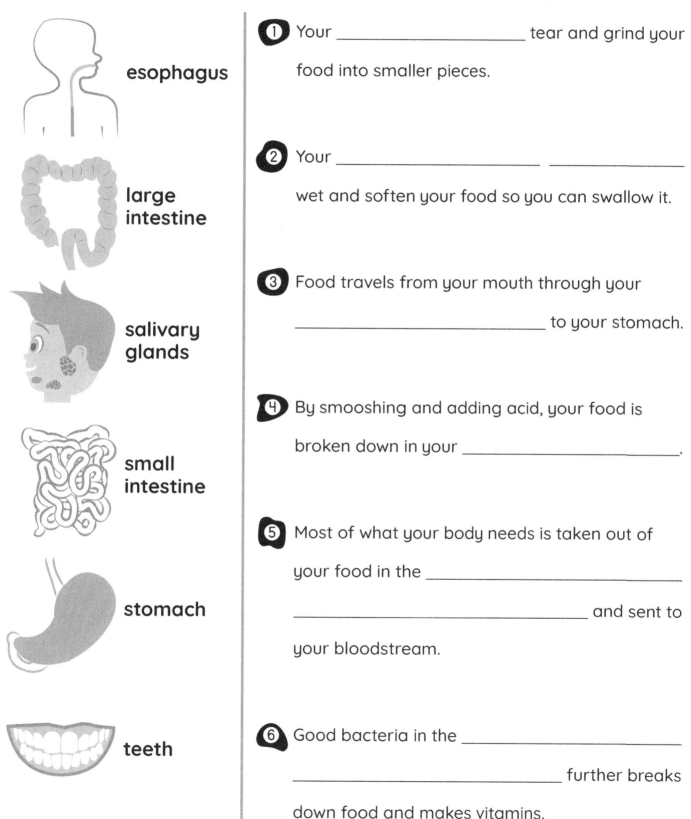

esophagus

large intestine

salivary glands

small intestine

stomach

teeth

① Your _____ tear and grind your food into smaller pieces.

② Your _____ _____ wet and soften your food so you can swallow it.

③ Food travels from your mouth through your _____ to your stomach.

④ By smooshing and adding acid, your food is broken down in your _____.

⑤ Most of what your body needs is taken out of your food in the _____ _____ and sent to your bloodstream.

⑥ Good bacteria in the _____ _____ further breaks down food and makes vitamins.

What About the Waste?

Feces aren't the only waste your body has to get rid of. Your body also makes **urine** (pee!). Your urinary system makes urine to remove waste from your blood.

GARBAGE REMOVAL

Your cells are **always** *working*, and they are always making waste. If this waste stayed in your body, it would make you very sick. As your blood moves around your body, it picks up cell waste like a garbage truck collecting trash.

Your body needs to take out its trash, and here is how it is done.

Most of the waste is removed from your blood by your bean-shaped **kidneys**. Kidneys are important filters.

Waste goes from the kidneys down a pair of tubes called **ureters** and into your bladder.

Your blood goes through your kidneys many times every day. Your pair of kidneys filter about **200 liters** of blood every day, even though you only have about **5 liters** in your body!

Your **bladder** is like a storage tank. When it is full, you get a *signal from your brain* that you need to go to the bathroom. You empty your bladder when you go to the bathroom. *You are taking out the trash!*

Serious Note: Your kidneys work all the time. If both of them stopped working, you would die in days, but you would be okay with just one kidney.

WOW!

Your kidneys will make about a swimming pool full of urine during your life!

Your Body Has a Filter

Find the Best Filter

Materials
- ☐ a cup
- ☐ plastic water bottle (no cap)

materials for "blood"
- ☐ 1 cup water
- ☐ $\frac{1}{8}$ tsp. glitter
- ☐ $\frac{1}{8}$ tsp. ground pepper
- ☐ $\frac{1}{8}$ tsp. colored drink mix

suggestions for filters
- ☐ gravel or dried beans
- ☐ sand
- ☐ paper towels
- ☐ cheesecloth
- ☐ coffee filters
- ☐ cotton balls
- ☐ fabric

Directions

① Ask a grown-up to cut the plastic water bottle as shown. Turn the top part, which will be the *kidney*, upside down and set it in the bottom part, the *bladder.*

② In a cup, mix together the water, drink mix, glitter, and pepper. This will represent *blood* with waste in it.

③ Your goal is to try to get as much "waste" out of the "blood" as possible by filtering it through the "kidney."

④ To start, choose one filtering material and place it into the upside-down water bottle. Pour the "blood" through your filter.

⑤ Observe the "blood" as it goes through the "kidney" filter into the "bladder."

How much waste did you remove? **some   most   all**

⑥ Try pouring the "blood" through the "kidney" filter again using a combination of filtering materials.

Which filters did you use? _____

How much waste did you remove this time? **some   most   all**

⑦ Keep trying different filter combinations.

What combination of filters worked best for you? _____

_____

Breathing—It Sounds Simple...

Take a deep breath **in** through your nose or your mouth. Hold it for a couple of seconds, then let it **out**. How do you do this? Your respiratory system is all about breathing! This system has two very important jobs—*moving oxygen* and *removing waste*!

Why We Breathe

The air we breathe has invisible *gases* in it. The cells in your body need a gas called **oxygen**. It is needed to turn sugar into energy. Without oxygen, your cells would die.

Your **respiratory system** brings in the oxygen your cells need. It also gets rid of a gas called **carbon dioxide** which is formed when your body turns sugar into energy. This gas can make you sick if there is too much in your body.

Breathe In—Inhale

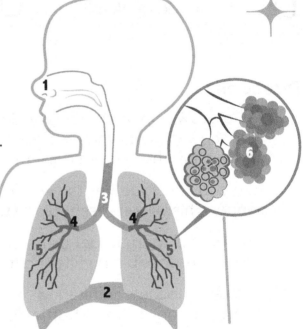

Directions: As you read about how you **inhale**, draw a red line on the diagram showing the path air takes going into your body.

1. Air comes in through your **nose** and **mouth**.

2. Your **diaphragm**, a large muscle between your chest and belly, is shaped a bit like a parachute. When you breathe, your diaphragm *contracts*, or moves down, and allows your lungs to get bigger.

3. Air goes down a tube called a **trachea**, or windpipe.

4. This tube splits into two branches called **bronchi**, which take air into each of your lungs.

5. In your lungs, air travels down branching tubes called **bronchioles**.

6. At the end of your bronchioles are very tiny air sacs called **alveoli**. Tiny **blood vessels** wrap around the alveoli. This is where the important work happens!

   Oxygen molecules move from your **alveoli** into your blood, where they are carried all over your body. *Carbon dioxide molecules* move from your blood into your alveoli.

Breathe Out—Exhale

Breathing out is called **exhaling**. Your diaphragm relaxes, which makes the air (full of carbon dioxide) go out of your lungs, through your trachea, and up to your mouth and nose.

WOW! Hiccups happen when your **diaphragm**, the large muscle under your lungs, contracts really quickly, making you suck in air. The world record for having the hiccups is **68 years**!

What do you do to stop the hiccups?

Directions: Use the words in the box to help you fill in the blanks. You will use some words more than once.

alveoli	bronchi	diaphragm	lungs	mouth	nose	trachea

1. Air goes in through your _____ and _____.

2. Your _____ *contracts*, expanding your _____.

3. The air goes down your _____, through your two _____, and into your _____.

4. In your _____, oxygen goes into your blood and carbon dioxide comes out.

5. Your _____ *relaxes* and air is pushed out of your lungs, up through your trachea, and out through your _____ and _____.

Counting Breaths

Materials   ☐ a timer   ☐ a pencil   ☐ a calculator

Directions

1. Sit quietly and set the timer for one minute. Have your pencil ready.
2. Start the timer and make a tally mark each time you **inhale** during the minute.

Tally		Total	

3. Calculate how many times you breathe in an hour and in a 24-hour day. (*Hint:* There are 60 minutes in an hour.)

   _____ breaths in an hour   _____ breaths in a day

4. You measured your breaths while you were sitting quietly. Try doing some jumping jacks and then counting your breaths again for one minute.

   What happens to the number of breaths? _____

   Why do you think this happens? _____

First Stop—Upper Airway

Directions: When you *inhale*, air first goes through your **upper airway**. Use the words in bold to help you label the diagram.

Your nose and sinuses have little hairs called **cilia** that trap dust and germs to keep them from going into your lungs.

Air comes in through your **nose**, and sometimes your **mouth**.

Your nose leads to your **sinuses**—spaces inside your head for air to pass through. Your sinuses and mouth also warm the air and make it moist.

The top part of your larynx is your **epiglottis**. It's a flap of tissue that covers your trachea, or windpipe, so that food and drink don't go into your lungs.

vocal cords

Your **larynx** is a tube-shaped ring of muscle connecting your upper and lower airways.

TRY THIS!

Can you breathe and swallow at the same time? No way! Your **epiglottis** opens when you breathe and always closes when you swallow. It also opens when you burp to let gases escape!

Inside your **larynx** are your vocal cords. They are like rubber bands stretched across your windpipe. When you talk or sing, air goes through your vocal cords and makes them *vibrate*, which makes sound.

So, why don't we make sounds when we breathe? **Answer:** When the vocal cords are relaxed, they don't vibrate!

Vocal Cord Model

Materials

☐ a plastic cup or small container

☐ a rubber band that can fit around the cup, top to bottom

Directions

1. Stretch the rubber band around the cup across the top and bottom.

2. Hold the cup upside down.

3. Take a deep breath and exhale, aiming your breath at the side of the rubber band. You might also try this blowing through a straw. *Note:* Adjust the angle of the straw until you hear a sound.

What's going on?

When you blow air across the rubber band, it *vibrates*, which makes a sound. This is a lot like when your breath goes across your vocal cords.

Directions: Draw lines to match the scientific words to their descriptions.

① **alveoli**

② **bronchi**

③ **cilia**

④ **diaphragm**

⑤ **epiglottis**

⑥ **larynx**

⑦ **trachea**

windpipe

flap of tissue covering the trachea

breathing tubes

dust-trapping hairs in your nose and sinuses

air sacs

large, dome-shaped muscle that contracts when you breathe in

voice box

Second Stop—Lower Airway

Your **lungs** are pink, spongy organs in your chest. Your left lung is a bit smaller than your right lung to make room for your **heart**. Your **ribs** protect your lungs and heart.

Your **lower airway** looks a bit like an upside-down tree with lots of branches. When you inhale, air goes through your **larynx** and down a tube called the **trachea**.

The **trachea**, or windpipe, splits into two branches called **bronchi**. One goes to your right lung and one goes to your left lung.

Tiny blood vessels called **capillaries** wrap around your **alveoli**.

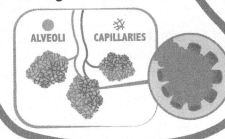

ALVEOLI   CAPILLARIES

Inside your lungs, the **bronchi** branch into lots of smaller and smaller tubes called **bronchioles**. At the end of every bronchiole are tiny bubble-like sacs called **alveoli**. They look like a bunch of teeny, tiny grapes.

WOW! You have about **600,000,000** (600 million) alveoli in your lungs!

The Gas Exchange

Oxygen molecules in the air you inhale go out of your alveoli and into your blood. They will be carried to cells all over your body.

At the same time, **carbon dioxide**—a molecule your body doesn't need—comes out of your blood and into your alveoli. Then you *exhale* (breathe out) the carbon dioxide.

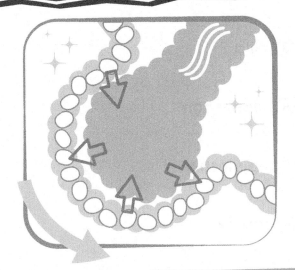

TEAM UP! Your respiratory and circulatory systems team up in your alveoli.

Lower Airway Model

Materials

☐ clear hard plastic 10-16 oz. bottle   ☐ scissors

☐ 2 round 8-inch balloons   ☐ utility knife
Safety Note: for adult to use only

Directions

1. Ask an adult to cut the bottle as shown. It should be cut so that the balloon hanging in it will have $\frac{3}{4}$ inch space below it.

   *The bottle will act as a model of your **ribcage**.*

2. Put one balloon partway into the neck of the bottle. Stretch the opening of the balloon over the neck of the bottle.

   *This balloon will be a model of a **lung**.*

3. Tie a knot in the second balloon. Cut the balloon across about $\frac{2}{3}$ of the way down from the opening.

4. Stretch the wide part of the balloon over the large opening of the bottle. Keep the knot on the outside.

   *This balloon will represent a **diaphragm** in your model.*

Work It!

1. To work your model, gently pull on the knot of the "diaphragm" and watch the "lung."

   What happens? _____

2. Gently push in on the "diaphragm."

   What happens? _____

3. How is this model like your real respiratory system? _____

   _____

   How is it different? _____

4. Can you recreate a hiccup or a cough with your model?   **yes**   **no**

   What did you try? _____

   Did it work?   yes   no

The Great Protectors!

Mucus, coughing, and sneezing don't seem like superheroes or protectors, but they are! Here is how they each protect you from germs.

Mucus

Do you ever get a runny nose? That gooey stuff is **mucus**, and it might be gross, but it has an important job! *Germs, dust,* and *dirt* in your body stick to mucus. When you blow your nose, it carries all that bad stuff out of your nose so it doesn't get to your lungs.

Healthy Habit Hint
Always blow your nose into a tissue and then wash your hands so you don't spread germs!

Sneezing

Your body has another trick to keep germs out of your lungs—**sneezing**! The purpose of a sneeze is to send germs out of your body. When you sneeze, a whole bunch of your muscles contract quickly and force air and germs out of your nose. Some of the muscles used to sneeze are your *diaphragm, chest muscles, belly muscles,* and *throat muscles.* Your *eyelids* always close when you sneeze.

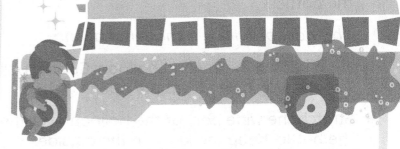

A sneeze can travel **100 miles per hour** and sneeze germs can travel the length of a school bus!

Healthy Habit Hint
Aways sneeze into a tissue or your elbow so you don't shoot germs all over everyone around you.

Coughing

What happens if pollen or dust **do** get into your trachea or lungs? You **cough**! Air comes out quickly, carrying out anything that is irritating your airway. Unlike sneezing or hiccupping, you can cough on purpose when you need to.

Healthy Habit Hint
Cover your mouth when you cough!

And what about yawning?

Another thing your body sometimes does automatically is **yawn**. You can also yawn on purpose. Why do we yawn? Nobody knows for sure!

Try this: Do a big, loud yawn. Watch the people around you. Do they yawn, too? Sometimes yawning is *contagious!*

Stop Those Germs!

Materials

☐ a towel ☐ glitter ☐ pen or pencil

☐ hand soap ☐ access to a sink

Preparation: Wash and dry your hands carefully. You want to learn about how germs spread *but not actually spread them!*

Directions

1. In this model, the glitter represents **germs**. We can't really see germs—they are too small! Sprinkle some glitter on your hands. Rub your hands together to get the "germs" all over them.

   What might cause germs to get all over your hands for real? _____

   _____

2. Shake hands with someone. What happens to the glitter germs? _____

   _____

3. Open a door and check the knob for glitter germs.
   Do you see any?   **yes**   **no**

4. Touch some other things that you use every day, such as your toys, video game controllers, TV remotes, or drawer handles.

   Did the germs go from your hands to the objects
   you touched?   **yes**   **no**

   How could someone else get those germs on their hands? _____

   _____

5. Most germs can't get into your body through your hands unless you have a cut or a sore. Your skin protects you. But germs can easily get into your respiratory system through your mouth and nose.

   How do germs do this?

   _____

6. Let's get rid of those germs! First, run some water over your hands.

   Did all of the "germs" wash away?   **yes**   **no**

7. Wash your hands again. This time, use soap and water.

   How long did it take for all the germs to wash away? _____

Around and Around It Goes

You have your own delivery system inside your body! It is called your **circulatory system**, and it delivers oxygen and food to all the parts of your body, just like a delivery person delivers packages.

Your **circulatory system** is made up of your **heart** and your **blood vessels**. Your heart squeezes, or beats, to move blood through all of your blood vessels. These tubes take blood all around your body.

WOW!

It takes less than a minute for blood to **circulate** from your heart, around your body, and back to your heart!

① First, your heart pumps blood to your lungs. There, it picks up oxygen.

② Then, your heart pumps fresh blood with lots of oxygen in it out to cells all over your body. When the blood reaches these cells, oxygen and food go into them.

③ **Waste**, like carbon dioxide, moves from your cells into your blood. Then, your circulatory system brings that blood back to your heart and your lungs, so it can be cleansed of waste and pick up fresh oxygen.

④ And around and around and around the blood goes!

To **circulate** means to *move around and around*. Your circulatory system moves blood around and around your body.

TEAM UP! Your heart and lungs are partners. They work together to bring in oxygen and remove carbon dioxide from your cells. Your kidneys also do important work to help your circulatory system. They clean waste and remove extra water from your blood.

88

Your Heart

Your **heart** is a very strong muscle. It beats, or squeezes, all the time, even when you are asleep. It can beat 100,000 times a day!

TRY THIS! Make a fist with your hand. Hold it up to your chest just to the left of the middle. This is about the size and placement of your heart.

Your heart is actually 2 pumps in one!

Your heart has four **chambers**, or rooms. The chambers on the *right* receive "old" blood from your body. The oxygen in this blood has been used up. It gets pumped to your lungs.

Color the chambers on the right blue (1).

The chambers on the *left* side receive *refreshed* blood full of oxygen from your lungs and then pump it out to your body.

Color the chambers on the left red (2).

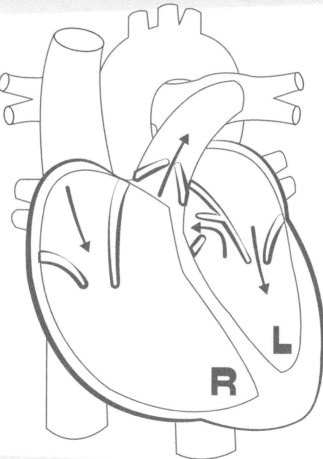

Each chamber has **valves** that keep blood going in one direction. The valves are like little doors that open to let blood move out, then close quickly so it doesn't come back in. As they open and close, they make the sound we hear as a *heartbeat*.

Color the valves green (3).

TRY THIS!

How strong is your heart muscle? Try squeezing a tennis ball hard enough to make it squish. That is how hard your heart works all the time! Can you squeeze the tennis ball once every second for 30 seconds?

To keep your heart muscle strong, do some exercise every day to increase your heart rate.

Check Your Heartbeat

Feel It!

Directions

1. Sit quietly.

2. Place two fingers on the side of your neck. You may need to move your fingers around just a bit until you find your pulse.

3. That *bomp-bomp, bomp-bomp* you feel is your heart moving blood through your blood vessels!

See It!

Materials

☐ a marshmallow (or small lump of clay or dough)

☐ a toothpick

Directions

1. Push the end of the toothpick into the marshmallow so that it sticks straight up.

2. Place the marshmallow on the inside of your wrist, below your thumb, with the toothpick sticking straight up. You may have to twist your arm just a little to get it to balance.

3. Watch the toothpick. Can you see it moving? That is your heartbeat!

Hear It!

Materials

☐ a funnel ☐ a paper towel tube ☐ tape ☐ a partner or family member

1. Stick the funnel into one end of the paper towel tube. Tape it in place.

2. Gently place the funnel against the left side of a partner's or a family member's chest. Place your ear against the end of the tube.

3. Listen to hear their heartbeat. How does it sound?

90

Calling All Engineers

The Mission: To build a *valve* in between two chambers that lets the blood flow one way, but stops it from flowing back in the other direction. Use any craft or building materials that you have on hand. Suggestions are provided.

Materials

- ☐ a shallow box or plastic bin
- ☐ cardboard
- ☐ scissors and tape (masking or duct tape)
- ☐ items that will roll or flow—marbles, dried beans, rice, etc.
- ☐ building materials—paper, index cards, tape, straws, craft sticks, string, foil, clay, etc.

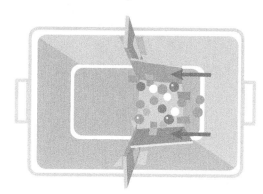

Directions

1. The box represents one side of your *heart*. You will use the cardboard to create a partial divider making two chambers in the heart.

2. Cut two pieces of cardboard and tape them in the middle of the long walls of the box, leaving a space between them for items to pass through.

3. The rolling or flowing items, such as marbles, dried beans, or rice, represent *blood cells*. Pour some "blood cells" into one side of the box. Tip the box back and forth so the "blood" flows between the chambers of the heart.

4. Use some building materials to build a valve (flap) across the opening. It should let blood flow in one direction but not move back in the other direction.

5. Did you stop all of the blood from going in the wrong direction? If not, make some changes to your design and try again!

6. Keep working on your valve until the blood flows only in one direction.

What's going on?

Your heart valves open to let blood flow forward through the chambers of your heart. They close to keep blood from flowing backward. Some people have problems with their heart valves. Their valves let some of their blood flow the wrong way, which makes them feel weak or short of breath. Doctors can put in artificial heart valves to help them.

Blood Transport

Blood vessels are tubes that carry blood around your body. You have three different kinds of blood vessels: arteries, veins, and capillaries.

WOW!

All your blood vessels together could wrap around Earth 2½ times (60,000 miles)!

Arteries are tubes that carry fresh oxygen-rich blood from your heart to your body. Arteries have *thick* walls and can stretch when lots of blood flows through them.
Color the arteries red.

Veins carry blood that needs oxygen from your body to your heart. They have *thin* walls and valves to keep blood from flowing backward. You might be able to see veins under your skin that look blue. They are really dark red.
Color the veins blue.

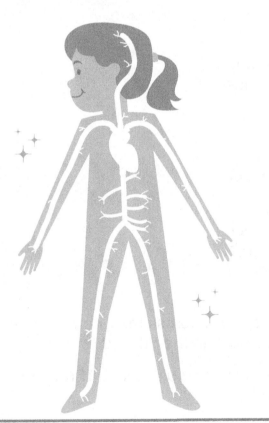
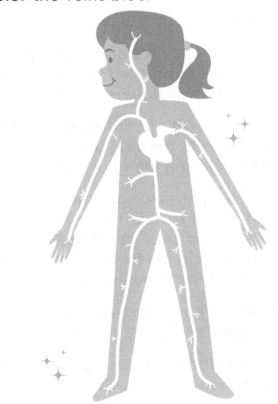

Capillaries are very tiny blood vessels that go to almost every cell in your body. You have over **10 million** capillaries!

Color the capillaries in the middle purple—a blending of red and blue.
Color the artery and capillaries on the left red.
Color the capillaries and vein on the right blue.

Your Blood

Depending on your size, you probably have between 11 and 13 cups of blood in your body. Your blood has three jobs:

1. Deliver oxygen to all your cells.
2. Remove carbon dioxide from your body.
3. Fight infections.

You know your blood is important. But what is blood made of? Blood has lots of different cells in it. It is sometimes called *liquid tissue*.

TRY THIS!

Measure 13 cups of water into a gallon jug to see how much blood you have in your body.

White blood cells are your protectors. They find and destroy germs and viruses, get rid of poisons, and take out dead or damaged cells.

55%, or just over half, of your blood is **plasma**. Blood plasma is a yellowish, watery liquid. It has important things that your cells need like water, nutrients, proteins, and salts. **Color the plasma yellow.**

Red blood cells make up about **44%** of your blood. Red blood cells carry oxygen to your cells. They look like squishy little dinner plates. **Color the red blood cells section red.**

Platelets are little pieces of cells that help stop bleeding. If you get a cut, platelets stick together and make a plug to stop the blood from coming out. This is called **blood clotting**. **Leave the white blood cells and platelets section white.**

WOW! Red blood cells make up **84%** of all the cells in your body. They only live about 120 days, so you need a steady supply of new ones. You make about 2 million new red blood cells in your bone marrow every second!

Blood in a Jar

Materials

- ☐ corn syrup (if you don't have any, you can use water with a little yellow food coloring in it)
- ☐ a small, clear jar with a lid
- ☐ a resealable bag
- ☐ O-shaped cereal
- ☐ red food coloring
- ☐ grains of rice
- ☐ small marshmallows

Directions

1. A little over half of your blood is plasma. Fill the jar just over halfway with corn syrup to represent *plasma*.

2. Add a few marshmallows to represent *white blood cells* and a few grains of rice to represent *platelets*. You only have one white blood cell for every 600 red blood cells, so don't add very many!

3. Now, let's make the red blood cells. Put some O-shaped cereal in a resealable bag and add some red food coloring. Shake the bag until the O-shaped cereal is red.

4. Fill your jar the rest of the way with "red blood cells."

5. Shake the bottle a bit to mix all the parts together. Now you have a model of your blood.

Answer Key

Page 7
1. Red blood cells and skin cells are very small and are parts of the body. They both have a cell membrane.
2. They are different colors, shapes, and sizes, and they do different jobs. A red blood cell does not have a nucleus or organelles.

Page 9
1. cell
2. tissue
3. organ
4. system

Page 12
1. lungs, respiratory system
2. brain, nervous system
3. heart, circulatory system
4. stomach, digestive system

Page 13
1. circulatory
2. nervous
3. digestive
4. respiratory
5. skeletal
6. muscular

Page 15
Skin Activity I: You might see lines, marks for hair, and flaky skin.

Page 19
Things skin does: protects your body; keeps moisture in; keeps germs and viruses out; helps you feel heat and pain; keeps your temperature from going too high or too low; grows hair

Page 20
Answers will vary.

Page 21
The child on the left is protected from sun damage; protective items include a hat, sunglasses, a long-sleeved shirt, an umbrella, and sunscreen.
Skin Activity 3: A possible explanation would be that the sunscreen protected the paper from fading.

Page 24
Answers will vary.

Page 25
Key:
1. Red (skull and jaw)
2. Blue (shoulder, arm, hand)
3. Green (ribs, spine)
4. Orange (pelvis, leg, foot)

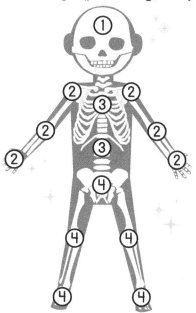

Page 26
1. blood vessels and nerves
2. compact
3. spongy
4. marrow

Page 27
Check that each bone of the cranium is colored a different color.
How many bones are in the skull altogether? 8 cranium bones + 14 facial bones = 22 skull bones. The only bone in your skull that moves is the jaw bone.
Checked activities: riding a bike, playing football, skateboarding, playing baseball

Page 29
7 bones in the cervical spine
12 bones in the thoracic spine
5 bones in the lumbar spine

Page 30
1. disc
2. vertebrae
3. ligaments
4. spinal cord

Page 32
54 hand bones altogether
52 foot bones altogether
106 bones in hands and feet altogether
Suggested answers:
1. Hands and feet need to make small, precise movements, so they have a lot of bones.
2. Foot bones are thicker and shorter, so they can carry the weight of your body.

Page 33
shoulder: ball-and-socket joint
cranium: fixed joint
knee: hinge joint

Page 34
1. Ligaments
2. Tendons

Page 38
Digesting your lunch—involuntary
Kicking a ball—voluntary
Moving blood around your body—involuntary
Smiling—voluntary

Page 41
Cerebrum—thinking, moving, sensing, learning, and remembering
Medulla—heartbeat, breathing
Cerebellum—movement, balance

Page 43
Yes, they have the same surface area.
No, they both can't fit in the same space.

Page 46
1. keep beating
2. move up and down to keep breathing
3. digest food

Page 47
Answers will vary.

Answer Key *(cont.)*

Page 49

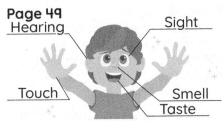

Hearing · Sight · Touch · Smell · Taste

Drawings will vary for each sense.

Page 50
1. Eyes sense light.
2. Ears sense sound waves.
3. The nose senses molecules in the air.
4. The tongue senses chemicals in food.
5. The skin senses surface textures.

Page 51
1. iris
2. pupil
3. retina
4. optic nerve
5. cornea
6. lens

Page 55
Answers will vary. One suggestion would be to lay pieces of paper above and below the thin, inside rectangle, blocking the shading of the outside rectangle. Then, one sees that the inner rectangle is all the same color.

Page 56
Answers will vary depending on food preferences.

Page 58
Answers will vary depending on food preferences.

Page 59
Answers will vary.

Page 61
Labels: outer ear, middle ear, inner ear

Page 70

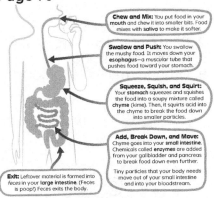

Chew and Mix: You put food in your mouth and chew it into smaller bits. Food mixes with saliva to make it softer.

Swallow and Push: You swallow the mushy food. It moves down your esophagus—a muscular tube that pushes food toward your stomach.

Squeeze, Squish, and Squirt: Your stomach squeezes and squishes the food into a soupy mixture called chyme (kime). Then, it squirts acid into the chyme to break the food down into smaller particles.

Add, Break Down, and Move: Chyme goes into your small intestine. Chemicals called enzymes are added from your gallbladder and pancreas to break food down even further. Tiny particles that your body needs move out of your small intestine and into your bloodstream.

Exit: Leftover material is formed into feces in your large intestine. (Feces is poop!) Feces exits the body.

1. <u>Enzymes</u> are chemicals in the small intestine used to break food down.
2. <u>Chyme</u> is a soupy food mixture created in the stomach.
3. <u>Saliva</u> is a mixture of water and chemicals, also called *spit*.

Page 71

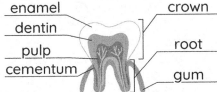

enamel · dentin · pulp · cementum · crown · root · gum

Page 73
32 adult (permanent) teeth – 20 baby teeth = 12 more adult teeth

Page 75
Check colors for parts of intestinal track.

Page 77
1. teeth
2. salivary glands
3. esophagus
4. stomach
5. small intestine
6. large intestine

Page 81
1. nose, mouth
2. diaphragm, lungs
3. trachea, bronchi, lungs
4. alveoli
5. diaphragm, mouth, nose

When you exercise your body needs more oxygen so you need to breathe more.

Page 82

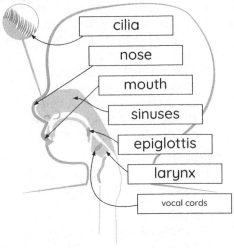

cilia · nose · mouth · sinuses · epiglottis · larynx · vocal cords

Page 83
1. alveoli—air sacs
2. bronchi—breathing tubes
3. cilia—dust-trapping hairs in your nose and sinuses
4. diaphragm—large, dome-shaped muscle
5. epiglottis—flap of tissue covering the trachea
6. larynx—voice box
7. trachea—windpipe

Page 92

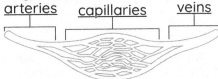

arteries · capillaries · veins

Page 93
Check colors for plasma (yellow) and red blood cells (red). The section for platelets should be white.

Made in the USA
Monee, IL
09 March 2024

54767281R00057